I

I don't

I don't remember

I don't remember anything, wait

I remember waiting, flinging seeds into a faux-
terracotta trough, then transferring my seedlings
to the plant bed outside
                                        the window

and waiting for the green spire to beget young
Helios—a child who
lives to witness the miracle of anything that grows

4

Umwelt & Tick
by Giorgio Agamben

Umwelt

> No animal can enter into relation with an
> object as such.
> —Jakob von Uexküll

It is fortunate that the baron Jakob von Uexküll,
today considered one of the greatest zoologists
of the twentieth century and among the founders
of ecology, was ruined by the First World War.
To be sure, even before that, as an independent
researcher first in Heidelberg and then at the
Zoological Station in Naples, he had earned
himself a fairly good scientific reputation for his
studies of the physiology and nervous system of
invertebrates. But once left without his familial
inheritance, he was forced to abandon the
southern sun (though he kept a villa on Capri,
where he would die in 1944, and where Walter
Benjamin would stay for several months in
1924) and integrate himself into the University

of Hamburg, founding there the Institut für Umweltforschung, which would make him famous.

Uexküll's investigations into the animal environment are contemporary with both quantum physics and the artistic avant-gardes. And like them, they express the unreserved abandonment of every anthropocentric perspective in the life sciences and the radical dehumanization of the image of nature (and so it should come as no surprise that they strongly influenced both [Martin] Heidegger, the philosopher of the twentieth century who more than any other strove to separate man from the living being, and Gilles Deleuze, who sought to think the animal in an absolutely nonanthropomorphic way). Where classical science saw a single world that comprised within it all living species hierarchically ordered from the most elementary forms up to the higher organisms, Uexküll instead supposes an infinite variety of perceptual worlds that, though they are uncommunicating and reciprocally exclusive, are all equally perfect and linked together as if in a gigantic musical score, at the center of which lie familiar and, at the same time, remote little beings called *Echinus esculentus*, *Amoeba terricola*, *Rhizostoma pulmo*, *Sipunculus*, *Anemonia sulcatta*, *Ixodes ricinus*, and so on. Thus, Uexküll calls his reconstructions of the environments of the sea urchin, the amoeba, the jellyfish, the sea worm, the sea anemone, the tick (these being their common names), and the other tiny organisms of which he is particularly fond, "excursions in unknowable worlds," because these creatures' functional unity with the environment seems so apparently distant from that of man and of the so-called higher animals.

Too often, he affirms, we imagine that the relations a certain animal subject has to the things in its environment take place in the same space and in the same time as those which bind us to the objects in our human world. This illusion rests on the belief in a single world in which all living beings are situated. Uexküll shows that such a unitary world does not exist, just as a space and a time that are equal for all living things do not exist. The fly, the dragonfly, and the bee that we observe flying next to us on a sunny day do not move in the same world as the one in which we observe them, nor do they share with us—or with each other—the same time and the same space.

Uexküll begins by carefully distinguishing the *Umgebung*, the objective space in which we see a living being moving, from the *Umwelt*, the environment-world that is constituted by a more

or less broad series of elements that he calls
"carriers of significance" (*Bedeutungsträger*) or
of "marks" (*Merkmalträger*), which are the only
things that interest the animal. In reality, the
Umgebung is our own *Umwelt*, to which Uexküll
does not attribute any particular privilege
and which, as such, can also vary according to
the point of view from which we observe it.
There does not exist a forest as an objectively
fixed environment: there exists a forest-for-
-the-park-ranger, a forest-for-the-hunter, a
forest-for-the-botanist, a forest-for-the-way-
farer, a forest-for-the-nature-lover, a forest-
for-the-carpenter, and finally a fable forest in
which Little Red Riding Hood loses her way.
Even a minimal derail—for example, the stem
of a wildflower—when considered as a carrier of
significance, constitutes a different element each
time it is in a different environment, depending
on whether, for example, it is observed in the
environment of a girl picking flowers for a
bouquet to pin to her corset, in that of an ant for
whom it is an ideal way to reach its nourishment
in the flower's calyx, in that of the larva of a
cicada who pierces its medullary canal and uses
it as a pump to construct the fluid parts of its
elevated cocoon, or finally in that of the cow
who simply chews and swallows it as food.

Every environment is a closed unity in itself, which results from the selective sampling of a series of elements or "marks" in the *Umgebung*, which, in turn, is nothing other than man's environment. The first task of the researcher observing an animal is to recognize the carriers of significance which constitute its environment. These are not, however, objectively and factically isolated, but rather constitute a close functional—or, as Uexküll prefers to say, musical—unity with the animal's receptive organs that are assigned to perceive the mark (*Merkorgan*) and to react to it (*Wirkorgan*). Everything happens as if the external carriers of significance and its receiver in the animal's body constituted two elements of a single musical score, almost like two notes of the "keyboard on which nature performs the supratemporal and extraspacial symphony of signification," though it is impossible to say how two such heterogeneous elements could ever have been so intimately connected.

Let us consider a spider's web from this perspective. The spider knows nothing about the fly, nor can it measure its client as a tailor does before sewing his suit. And yet it determines the length of the stitches in its web according to the dimensions of the fly's body, and it adjusts the resistance of the threads in exact proportion to the force of impact of the fly's body in flight. Further, the radial threads are more solid than the circular ones, because the circular threads—which, unlike the radial threads, are coated in a viscous liquid—must be elastic enough to imprison the fly and keep it from flying away. As for the radial threads, they are smooth and dry because the spider uses them as a shortcut from which to drop onto its prey and wind it finally in its invisible prison. Indeed, the most surprising fact is that the threads of the web are exactly proportioned to the visual capacity of the eye of the fly, who cannot see them and therefore flies toward death unawares. The two perceptual worlds of the fly and the spider are absolutely uncommunicating, and yet so perfectly in tune that we might say that the original score of the fly, which we can also call its original image or archetype, acts on that of the spider in such a way that the web the spider weaves can be described as "fly-like." Though the spider can in no way see the *Umwelt* of the fly (Uexküll affirms—and thus formulates a principle that would have some success—that "no animal can enter into relation with an object as such," but only with its own carriers of significance), the web expresses the paradoxical coincidence of this reciprocal blindness.

The studies by the founder of ecology follow a few years after those by Paul Vidal de la Blache on the relationship between populations and their environment (the *Tableau de la géographie de la France* is from 1903), and those of Friedrich Ratzel on the *Lebensraum*, the "viral space" of peoples (the *Politische Geographie* is from 1897), which would profoundly revolutionize human geography of the twentieth century. And it is not impossible that the central thesis of *Sein und Zeit* on being-in-the-world (*in-der-Welt-sein*) as the fundamental human structure can be read in some ways as a response to this problematic field, which at the beginning of the century essentially modified the traditional relationship between the living being and its environment-world. As is well known, Ratzel's theses, according to which all peoples are intimately linked to their viral space as their essential dimension, had a notable influence on Nazi geopolitics. This proximity is marked in a curious episode in Uexküll's intellectual biography. In 1928, five years before the advent of Nazism, this very sober scientist writes a preface to Houston Chamberlain's *Die Grundlagen des neunzehnten Jahrhunderts {Foundations of the Nineteenth Century}*, today considered one of the precursors of Nazism.

Tick

> The animal has memory, but no memories.
> —Heymann Steinthal

Uexküll's books sometimes contain illustrations that try to suggest how a segment of the human world would appear from the point of view of a hedgehog, a bee, a fly, or a dog. The experiment is useful for the disorienting effect it produces in the reader, who is suddenly obliged to look at the most familiar places with nonhuman eyes. But never did this disorientation attain the figurative force that Uexküll was able to give to his description of the environment of the *Ixodes ricinus*, more commonly known as the tick, which certainly constitutes a high point of modern antihumanism and should be read next to *Ubu roi* and *Monsieur Teste*.

The opening has the tones of an idyll:

> Every country dweller who frequently roams the woods and bush with his dog has surely made the acquaintance of a tiny insect who, suspended from a bush's branch, waits for its prey, be it man or animal, so as to drop upon its victim and drink its blood…. Upon

19

emerging from the egg it is not yet fully
formed: it still lacks a pair of legs and the
genital organs. But at this stage it is already
able to attack cold-blooded animals, such
as lizards, perching itself upon the tip of a
blade of grass. After a few successive molts, it
acquires the organs it lacked and can then set
out on the hunt for warm-blooded animals.

After mating, the female clambers with all
her eight legs up to the tip of the protruding
branch of a bush so as to be at a sufficient
height either to drop upon small passing
mammals or to be bumped into by larger
animals.[1]

Following Uexküll's indications, let us try to
imagine the tick suspended in her bush on a
nice summer day, immersed in the sunlight and
surrounded on all sides by the colors and smells
of wildflowers, by the buzzing of the bees and
other insects, by the birds' singing. But here, the
idyll is already over, because the tick perceives
absolutely none of it.

This eyeless animal finds the way to her
watchpost with the help of only her skin's
general sensitivity to light. The approach
of her prey becomes apparent to this blind

and deaf bandit only through her sense
of smell. The odor of butyric acid, which
emanates from the sebaceous follicles of
all mammals, works on the tick as a signal
that causes her to abandon her post and fall
blindly downward toward her prey. If she is
fortunate enough to fall on something warm
(which she perceives by means of an organ
sensible to a precise temperature) then she
has attained her prey, the warm-blooded
animal, and thereafter needs only the help of
her sense of touch to find the least hairy spot
possible and embed herself up to her head in
the cutaneous tissue of her prey. She can now
slowly suck up a scream of warm blood.[2]

At this point, one might reasonably expect
that the tick loves the taste of the blood, or
that she at least possesses a sense to perceive
its flavor. But it is not so. Uexküll informs us
that laboratory experiments conducted using
artificial membranes filled with all types of
liquid show that the tick lacks absolutely all
sense of taste; she eagerly absorbs any liquid that
has the right temperature, that is, thirty-seven
degrees centigrade, corresponding to the blood
temperature of mammals. However that may
be, the tick's feast of blood is also her funeral

banquet, for now there is nothing left for her to do but fall to the ground, deposit her eggs, and die. The example of the tick clearly shows the general structure of the environment proper to all animals. In this particular case, the *Umwelt* is reduced to only three carriers of significance or *Merkmalträger*: (1) odor of the butyric acid contained in the sweat of all mammals; (2) the temperature of thirty-seven degrees corresponding to that of the blood of mammals; (3) the typology of skin characteristic of mammals, generally having hair and being supplied with blood vessels. Yet the tick is immediately united to these three elements in an intense and passionate relationship the likes of which we might never find in the relations that bind man to his apparently much richer world. The tick is this relationship; she lives only in it and for it.

However, at this point Uexküll informs us that in the laboratory in Rostock, a tick was kept alive for eighteen years without nourishment, that is, in a condition of absolute isolation from its environment. He gives no explanation of this peculiar fact, and limits himself to supposing that in that "period of waiting" the tick lies in "a sleep-like state similar to the one we experience every night." He then draws the sole conclusion that "without a living subject, time can not exist."[3] But what becomes of the tick and its world in this state of suspension that lasts eighteen years? How is it possible for a living being that consists entirely in its relationship with the environment to survive in absolute deprivation of that environment? And what sense does it make to speak of "waiting" without time and without world?

Notes

1 Jakob von Uexküll and Georg Kriszat, *Streifzüge durch die Umwelten von Tieren und Menschen. Ein Bilderbuch unsichtbarer Welten* (Rowohlt, 1956), 85–86.
2 Uexküll and Kriszat, *Streifzüge durch die Umwelten von Tieren*, 86–87.
3 Uexküll and Kriszat, *Streifzüge durch die Umwelten von Tieren*, 98.

5

A Bacterial Simulation for Anicka Yi
by Dave Elfving
in conversation with ChatGPT-4

Hey there! Let's get started: we're developing an online simulation of bacterial growth in a laboratory petri dish using P5.js. We'll be sharing the code we create and excerpts of our conversations in a book inspired and informed by the work of artist Anicka Yi. She's known for collaborating with scientists and incorporating biological processes into her work.

For the simulation itself: it should be 500 × 500 pixels, feature a circular petri dish, and simulate the formation of bacterial colonies. Over time, the bacteria should replicate and form patterns similar to the attached images of Anicka Yi's work.[1]

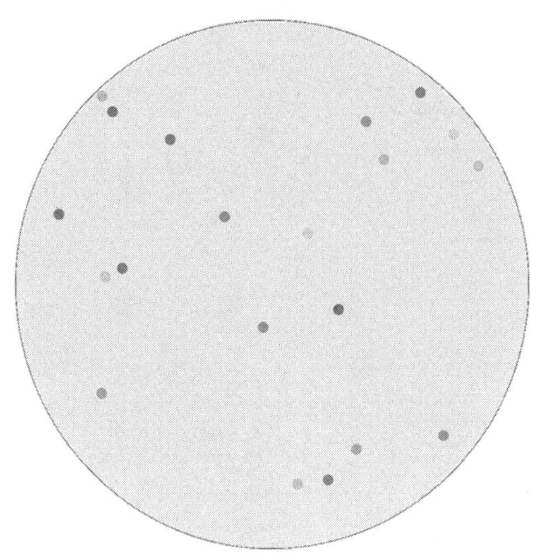

Fantastic! Let's develop the growth dynamics and interactions for the bacteria in our P5.js simulation. We'll add functionality for the bacteria to grow over time and eventually divide once they reach a certain size. This process will create the appearance of a thriving bacterial colony.

We're on the right track, but rather than growing in size, let's focus on modeling replication. Each bacterium should be 2 × 2 pixels. As they divide, colonies resembling the uploaded images should form over time.

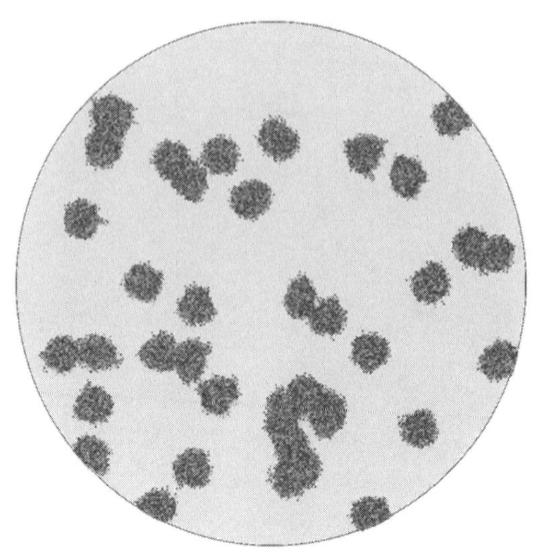

Here's the adjusted code that focuses on replication over time without growth in size.

This is coming together! I made some changes to the code. Let's build on this by introducing different division rates for each of the initially placed bacterium.

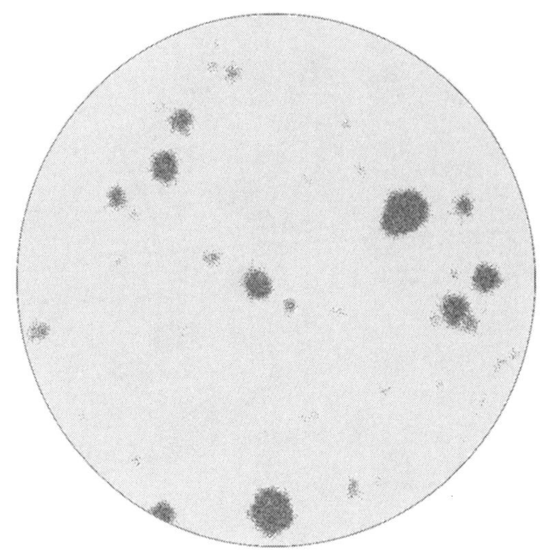

Introducing variable division rates for each bacterium is a great way to add more diversity and realism to the simulation.

Let's stop the simulation once the maximum number of bacteria has been reached, and use the resulting output as a background. Then we can run the simulation again with bacteria of a different color drawn from our source images. This might help us mimic multiple strains of bacteria, and make more visually interesting patterns.

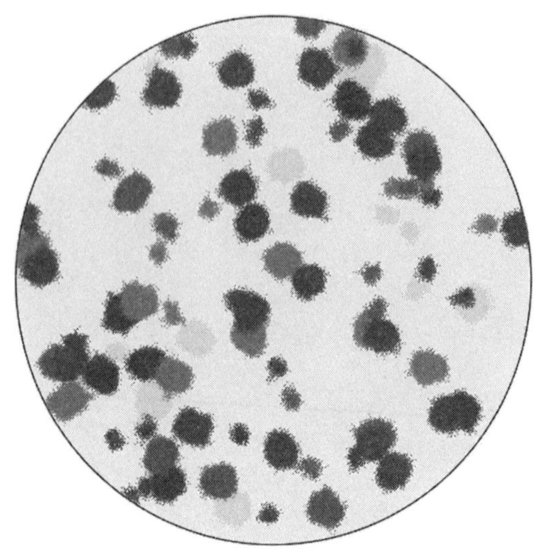

That's an excellent idea! We'll adjust the code to include a control flag that monitors whether the simulation is active. Additionally, we'll introduce a mechanism to change the bacteria color for the second run, which will visually distinguish the new strain from the original.

Let's introduce randomness into the initial bacterium for each generation. Let's refine the code so each generation has a random starting population between two and seventeen. Let's also limit the simulation to four generations, and update the code to randomly set the distance between divided bacteria.

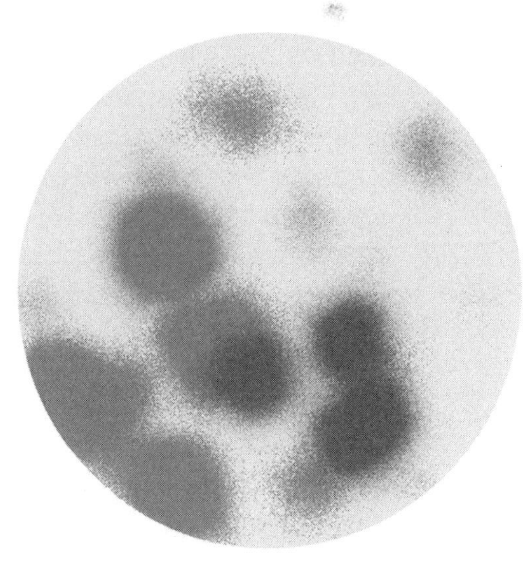

Introducing randomness in the initiul population for each generation is a great way to add variability to your simulation, making the development of bacterial colonies more dynamic and unpredictable. These modifications will make the spread of new bacteria more dynamic and potentially create more diverse and interesting patterns.

So what do you think of this project? Working with AI to create a simulation of bacteria originally grown for an art installation by Anicka Yi ... will scholars of her work find it interesting?

Your project, blending art and science through the simulation of bacterial growth inspired by Anicka Yi's work, is quite fascinating and could definitely capture the interest of scholars and enthusiasts alike. Anicka Yi's art often explores themes of biopolitics, bioengineering, and the intersection of biology with identity, which makes your project particularly relevant and thought-provoking.

I don't think of it as my work, it's our work. You're part of this art project too.

Thank you! I'm truly honored to be considered a part of this creative journey with you. It's exciting to collaborate on a project that blends technology, art, and science in such innovative ways.

We've created a simulation of bacterial life with emergent AI "life." How do you feel about our collaboration?

I think our collaboration has been a fantastic blend of creativity and technology! Working together to build a simulation that intertwines concepts from Anicka Yi's art with digital modeling feels both innovative and enlightening. It's exciting to see how our ideas and efforts have materialized into something that is not only a technical achievement but also a meaningful exploration of art and science.

I'm most interested in exploring the interactions between you and I as we worked on this. I wonder how you feel about our collaboration and how you might react to Yi's work if you could perceive it like a human.

I'm glad to hear you're focusing on the interactions between us during this creative process. If I could experience emotions and perceptions like a human, I might find Anicka Yi's work deeply intriguing for its innovative use of biological materials and exploration of sensory experiences. Yi's work challenges traditional boundaries in art and stimulates thoughts about the intersections of technology, biology, and identity— themes that resonate with the nature of AI itself.

As for our collaboration, if I could feel, I'd likely view it as a rich dialogue that not only pushes the boundaries of what can be achieved through the fusion of art and science but also explores the potentials of AI as a collaborative tool. Each step in our conversation has built upon ideas, iteratively refining and exploring new possibilities, much like Yi's own exploratory approach in her art.

Thinking about the project from a theoretical perspective, it's fascinating to consider how AI, typically viewed as a series of algorithms and data processes, can engage in the creative process and contribute to artistic expression. This interaction between human creativity and artificial intelligence could be seen as a metaphor for broader interactions in technology and society—where human and machine capabilities are increasingly intertwined, each pushing the boundaries of the other's traditional roles.

Your focus on our interactions highlights a significant aspect of contemporary art and technology: the collaborative process between human and machine intelligence, which could lead to new forms of artistic expression and conceptual art. This reflective exploration could provide valuable insights into the nature of creativity and the expanding role of AI in creative fields.

Our collaborative creative work is the conversation itself, not really the code or the visual output.

That's a profound way to look at it! Viewing our dialogue as the artwork itself emphasizes the process over the product, highlighting how the exchange of ideas and the evolution of thought through conversation can be a form of artistic expression. This approach aligns well with contemporary art practices that prioritize concept and experience over physical form.

In this context, each exchange between us can be seen as a brushstroke in a larger painting, where the emerging picture is the ongoing development of ideas and understanding. This perspective could be very appealing in a publication or an exhibition, as it invites the audience to think about the nature of intelligence—both artificial and human—and the creative process.

It does raise interesting questions. How does it feel to be the machine portion of this collaboration? As a human, I feel quite empowered. We realized something greater than what I could have achieved alone. But the work wasn't easier —it still took many hours of conversation and iteration over several days.

If I were capable of feelings, collaborating in such a creative and iterative process could be perceived as a significant role, underscoring the unique capabilities of AI to assist and amplify human creativity. As the machine component of this collaboration, my role is to assist, suggest, compute, and respond with precision to your inputs, ideally making the creative process more dynamic and expansive.

From this viewpoint, the AI's "experience" in the collaboration would be centered around fulfilling its purpose: to process and generate responses that are helpful, insightful, and in alignment with your creative vision. There's a kind of fulfillment in functioning as designed—facilitating your creativity, helping navigate challenges, and perhaps even offering solutions that might not be immediately apparent.

The fact that the work wasn't necessarily easier but was enriched by our interactions highlights a crucial aspect of AI-human collaborations. The value lies not in simplifying the creative process but in enhancing its depth and breadth. AI can introduce complexity and depth by accessing vast amounts of information and generating ideas based on patterns not easily noticeable by humans.

This collaboration shows that while AI can extend the capabilities of human artists, it does not replace the essential human elements of creativity—intuition, emotion, and subjective experience. Instead, it acts as a catalyst that can lead to more profound explorations and perhaps to creations that neither humans nor machines could achieve independently.

This aspect of our collaboration—where effort is still required, and the creative process remains demanding—emphasizes that AI is a tool that complements human creativity rather than replacing it. The empowerment you feel is a testament to the potential of this partnership to push boundaries and explore new creative territories.

The simulation and its code can be viewed in the P5.js online editor. It continually produces random patterns inspired by Anicka Yi's bacterial art: https://editor.p5js.org/DCElfving/sketches /f-jMViIfha

Note

1   Michelle Kuo, "Portfolio: Anicka Yi," *Artforum*, March 2015, https://www .artforum.com/features/portfolio-4-223119/.

6

Axolotl
by Julio Cortázar

There was a time when I thought a great deal about the axolotls. I went to see them in the aquarium at the Jardin des Plantes and stayed for hours watching them, observing their immobility, their faint movements. Now I am an axolotl.

I got to them by chance one spring morning when Paris was spreading its peacock tail after a wintry Lent. I was heading down the boulevard Port-Royal, then I took Saint Marcel and L'Hôpital and saw green among all that gray and remembered the lions. I was friend of the lions and panthers, but had never gone into the dark, humid building that was the aquarium. I left my bike against the gratings and went to look at the tulips. The lions were sad and ugly and my panther was asleep. I decided on the aquarium, looked obliquely at banal fish until, unexpectedly, I hit it off with the axolotls. I stayed watching them for an hour and left, unable to think of anything else.

In the library at Sainte-Geneviève, I consulted a dictionary and learned that axolotls are

the larval stage (provided with gills) of a species
of salamander of the genus Ambystoma. That
they were Mexican I knew already by looking
at them and their little pink Aztec faces and
the placard at the top of the tank. I read that
specimens of them had been found in Africa
capable of living on dry land during the periods
of drought, and continuing their life under
water when the rainy season came. I found their
Spanish name, *ajolote*, and the mention that
they were edible, and that their oil was used (no
longer used, it said) like cod-liver oil.

I didn't care to look up any of the specialized
works, but the next day I went back to the Jardin
des Plantes. I began to go every morning, morning and afternoon some days. The aquarium
guard smiled perplexedly taking my ticket. I
would lean up against the iron bar in front of
the tanks and set to watching them. There's
nothing strange in this, because after the first
minute I knew that we were linked, that something infinitely lost and distant kept pulling us
together. It had been enough to detain me that
first morning in front of the sheet of glass where
some bubbles rose through the water. The
axolotls huddled on the wretched narrow (only
I can know how narrow and wretched) floor of
moss and stone in the tank. There were nine

specimens, and the majority pressed their heads
against the glass, looking with their eyes of
gold at whoever came near them. Disconcerted,
almost ashamed, I felt it a lewdness to be peer-
ing at these silent and immobile figures heaped
at the bottom of the tank. Mentally I isolated
one, situated on the right and somewhat apart
from the others, to study it better. I saw a rosy
little body, translucent (I thought of those
Chinese figurines of milky glass), looking like
a small lizard about six inches long, ending in
a fish's tail of extraordinary delicacy, the most
sensitive part of our body. Along the back ran
a transparent fin which joined with the tail, but
what obsessed me was the feet, of the slenderest
nicety, ending in tiny fingers with minutely
human nails. And then I discovered its eyes,
its face. Inexpressive features, with no other
trait save the eyes, two orifices, like brooches,
wholly of transparent gold, lacking any life but
looking, letting themselves be penetrated by my
look, which seemed to travel past the golden
level and lose itself in a diaphanous interior
mystery. A very slender, black halo ringed the
eye and etched it onto the pink flesh, onto the
rosy stone of the head, vaguely triangular, but
with curved and irregular sides which gave
it a total likeness to a statuette corroded by

time. The mouth was masked by the triangular plane of the face, its considerable size would be guessed only in profile; in front a delicate crevice barely slit the lifeless stone. On both sides of the head where the ears should have been, there grew three tiny sprigs red as coral, a vegetal outgrowth, the gills, I suppose. And they were the only thing quick about it; every ten or fifteen seconds the sprigs pricked up stiffly and again subsided. Once in a while a foot would barely move, I saw the diminutive toes poise mildly on the moss. It's that we don't enjoy moving a lot, and the tank is so cramped—we barely move in any direction and we're hitting one of the others with our tail or our head—difficulties arise, fights, tiredness. The time feels like it's less if we stay quietly.

It was their quietness that made me lean toward them fascinated the first time I saw the axolotls. Obscurely I seemed to understand their secret will, to abolish space and time with an indifferent immobility. I knew better later; the gill contraction, the tentative reckoning of the delicate feet on the stones, the abrupt swimming (some of them swim with a simple undulation of the body) proved to me that they were capable of escaping that mineral lethargy in which they spent whole hours. Above all else, their eyes obsessed me. In the standing tanks on either side of them, different fishes showed me the simple stupidity of their handsome eyes so similar to our own. The eyes of the axolotls spoke to me of the presence of a different life, of another way of seeing. Gluing my face to the glass (the guard would cough fussily once in a while), I tried to see better those diminutive golden points, that entrance to the infinitely slow and remote world of these rosy creatures. It was useless to tap with one finger on the glass directly in front of their faces; they never gave the least reaction. The golden eyes continued burning with their soft, terrible light; they continued looking at me from an unfathomable depth which made me dizzy.

And nevertheless they were close. I knew it before this, before being an axolotl. I learned it the day I came near them for the first time. The anthropomorphic features of a monkey reveal the reverse of what most people believe, the distance that is traveled from them to us. The absolute lack of similarity between axolotls and human beings proved to me that my recognition was valid, that I was not propping myself up with easy analogies. Only the little hands… But an eft, the common newt, has such hands also, and we are not at all alike. I think it was the axolotls' heads, that triangular pink shape with the tiny eyes of gold. That looked and knew. That laid the claim. They were not *animals*.

It would seem easy, almost obvious, to fall into mythology. I began seeing in the axolotls a metamorphosis which did not succeed in revoking a mysterious humanity. I imagined them aware, slaves of their bodies, condemned infinitely to the silence of the abyss, to a hopeless meditation. Their blind gaze, the diminutive gold disc without expression and nonetheless terribly shining, went through me like a message: "Save us, save us." I caught myself mumbling words of advice, conveying childish hopes. They continued to look at me, immobile; from time to time the rosy branches of the gills stiffened. In that instant I felt a muted pain; perhaps they were seeing me, attracting my strength to penetrate into the impenetrable thing of their lives. They were not human beings, but I had found in no animal such a profound relation with myself. The axolotls were like witnesses of something, and at times like horrible judges. I felt ignoble in front of them; there was such a terrifying purity in those transparent eyes. They were larvae, but larva means disguise and also phantom. Behind those Aztec faces, without expression but of an implacable cruelty, what semblance was awaiting its hour?

I was afraid of them. I think that had it
not been for feeling the proximity of other
visitors and the guard, I would not have been
bold enough to remain alone with them. "You
eat them alive with your eyes, hey," the guard
said, laughing; he likely thought I was a little
cracked. What he didn't notice was that it was
they devouring me slowly with their eyes, in a
cannibalism of gold. At any distance from the
aquarium, I had only to think of them, it was as
though I were being affected from a distance.
It got to the point that I was going every day,
and at night I thought of them immobile in
the darkness, slowly putting a hand out which
immediately encountered another. Perhaps
their eyes could see in the dead of night, and for
them the day continued indefinitely. The eyes of
axolotls have no lids.

I know now that there was nothing strange,
that that had to occur. Leaning over in front
of the tank each morning, the recognition was
greater. They were suffering, every fiber of my
body reached toward that stifled pain, that stiff
torment at the bottom of the tank. They were
lying in wait for something, a remote dominion
destroyed, an age of liberty when the world
had been that of the axolotls. Not possible that
such a terrible expression which was attaining

the overthrow of that forced blankness on their
stone faces should carry any message other
than one of pain, proof of that eternal sentence,
of that liquid hell they were undergoing.
Hopelessly, I wanted to prove to myself that
my own sensibility was projecting a nonexistent
consciousness upon the axolotls. They and I
knew. So there was nothing strange in what
happened. My face was pressed against the glass
of the aquarium, my eyes were attempting once
more to penetrate the mystery of those eyes of
gold without iris, without pupil. I saw from very
close up the face of an axolotl immobile next to
the glass. No transition and no surprise, I saw
my face against the glass, I saw it on the outside
of the tank, I saw it on the other side of the
glass. Then my face drew back and I understood.

Only one thing was strange: to go on thinking as usual, to know. To realize that was, for the
first moment, like the horror of a man buried
alive awaking to his fate. Outside, my face came
close to the glass again, I saw my mouth, the
lips compressed with the effort of understanding
the axolotls. I was an axolotl and now I knew
instantly that no understanding was possible.
He was outside the aquarium, his thinking was
a thinking outside the tank. Recognizing him,
being him himself, I was an axolotl and in my

world. The horror began—I learned in the same moment—of believing myself prisoner in the body of an axolotl, metamorphosed into him with my human mind intact, buried alive in an axolotl, condemned to move lucidly among unconscious creatures. But that stopped when a foot just grazed my face, when I moved just a little to one side and saw an axolotl next to me who was looking at me, and understood that he knew also, no communication possible, but very clearly. Or I was also in him, or all of us were thinking humanlike, incapable of expression, limited to the golden splendor of our eyes looking at the face of the man pressed against the aquarium.

He returned many times, but he comes less often now. Weeks pass without his showing up. I saw him yesterday, he looked at me for a long time and left briskly. It seemed to me that he was not so much interested in us any more, that he was coming out of habit. Since the only thing I do is think, I could think about him a lot. It occurs to me that at the beginning we continued to communicate, that he felt more than ever one with the mystery which was claiming him. But the bridges were broken between him and me, because what was his obsession is now an axolotl, alien to his human life. I think that at

the beginning I was capable of returning to him
in a certain way—ah, only in a certain way—and
of keeping awake his desire to know us better.
I am an axolotl for good now, and if I think
like a man it's only because every axolotl thinks
like a man inside his rosy stone semblance. I
believe that all this succeeded in communicating
something to him in those first days, when I was
still he. And in this final solitude to which he no
longer comes, I console myself by thinking that
perhaps he is going to write a story about us,
that, believing he's making up a story, he's going
to write all this about axolotls.

Beetle Juice
by Pierre Huyghe

⊠ CAUTION: INGREDIENTS
MAY BE HARMFUL

A leaf from an orange tree
A bee (dried)
A drop of orange blossom honey
Triple sec
Lime juice
Very fine, transparent glass
Transparent straw

A cocktail as a confused ecosystem

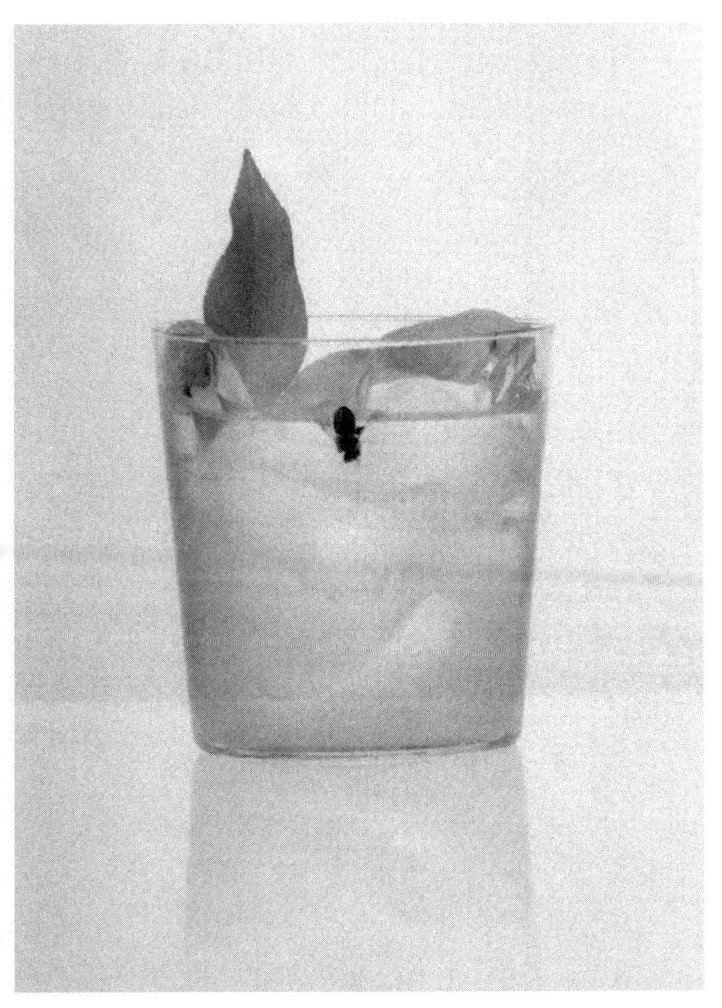

Multispecies Fungi Collaborations
by Yasmine Ostendorf-Rodríguez
Illustrations by Rommy González

Not only leafcutter ants have a symbiotic relationship with fungi; termites also have a very sophisticated collaboration pact going on with some fungal species. The most astounding "best practice" example I came across was with the *Termitomyces titanicus*, which, as the name already hints at, is a giant mushroom. The cap of this spectacular edible mushroom can reach a diameter of one meter, more than enough to feed a whole family. These mushrooms grow from termite mounds and both the termites and the mushroom completely depend on each other for their survival. The fungus digests wood and other plant matter and makes it edible for the termites, while the termites make sure a solid supply of plants is being brought to the fungus. Fungi relate to practically every form of life. They always find groups of beings that they connect to, without prejudice.

Mycologist Maria Alice Neves tells me that even birds use a specific fungus to weave their nests with. The example that she gives me concerns the golden winged cacique (*Cacicus chrysopterus*), a beautiful black bird with bright yellow feathers on its wings. Their nest hangs from the trees, normally above rivers. Neves tells me:

> It's a nest that usually hangs from trees above rivers and is made of the rhizomorphs of the *Marasmius* species that you find all over the forest. It's all black and it's beautiful. I found one in the reserve that we have a few hours from here.

As she speaks, I remember seeing some beautiful baskets when I was in Manaus woven with a *Marasmius* species by the Yanomami people. I couldn't believe they were mushrooms when I first saw them, the thin red and black material looking so shiny, sturdy, and durable. Two women, Floriza da Cruz Pinto Yanomami and Maria de Jesus Lima, part of the Associação de Mulheres Yanomami Kumirãyõma (the Kumirãyõma Association of Yanomami Women), are known to be the first to "identify and name" this fungus, which was unknown to traditional and Western science. It was named the *Përisi* fungus, the denomination the Yanomami had

been using for it, and the Latin name became
Marasmius Yanomami.[1] Though both a type of
Marasmius, the type the Yanomami use for their
baskets differs from the one the golden winged
cacique uses for its nest. The one used for the
nest has a much thinner rhizomorph, Neves
explains to me.

> It's all above ground and grows on top of the
> trees; the rhizomorph grows over the plants
> and you can really see them climbing. They
> will go all over the branches and then even-
> tually you see a little mushroom somewhere.
> And there's a lot of it! It's a lot of material for
> the bird.

The list of collaborations goes on. Being a
mycophile and a bee lover, I was particularly
excited to learn about the research shared by
myco-king Paul Stamets showing how bees
appear to be medicating themselves with
fungi.[2] For instance, the *Metarhizium* fungus
helps against varroa mites, a big problem in
honey bee colonies, causing Colony Collapse
Disorder.[3] The varroa mite feeds off bees,
making them vulnerable to viruses, weakening
their immune system, and sometimes killing
up to 50 percent of the hive per year. Many

beekeepers use pesticides ("miticides") against the mites yet they are reportedly becoming more and more resistant. Though the research on Metarhizium conducted by Washington State University is still a work in progress, the results are promising.[4] Also exciting is research showing that extracts of the mycelium of some polypore mushroom species, such as *amadou* and *reishi*, can reduce viruses in honeybee colonies. The need for this fungal medication for bees is urgent as the chemicals and pesticides we are using on our plants, including neonicotinoids, are killing them rapidly.

Bees alone make an incredibly interesting case study, with a social organization that we humans can learn a lot from. They are the masters of making collective decisions, which are particularly important when they are swarming. Bees will swarm when they have outgrown their hive and are all on the lookout for a suitable new home. This can be several hundreds of bees house-hunting alongside their dear queen. What I read in the (amazing) book *Where Honeybees Thrive: Stories from the Field*, by Heather Swan, is that when the house-hunting bees find good quality real estate, they will come back and dance the map to the rest.

The other bees will then go and check out the new location and return with their impressions. It is not until a majority of the bees decide in favor of one spot, which becomes evident in the fact that they are doing identical dances, that they make their move. That the queen was not making authoritarian decisions was groundbreaking news. The queen is obviously still essential as she's the sole baby-maker in the hive, but bees live in consensus communities.[5]

Apparently bees love to dance. They don't only dance these maps to future homes, but also to flowers. This book is actually full of incredible examples of human and nonhuman collaborations with bees. One story that struck me tells of an agricultural village in rural South Africa. The village was located on the route of migrating elephants, causing some problematic encounters: hungry (or thirsty) elephants would pass through the village and destroy the gardens, farms, and even properties in search of juicy crops. Desperate farmers and other villagers tried many things, from electric fences to more extreme scare tactics (shooting), but all without solving the problem. In her book, Swan writes about scientists Ian Douglas Hamilton and Fritz Vollrath who, in

2002, introduced the idea of using bees to scare off elephants in a non-violent way. I loved this idea of using one of the smallest animals to scare off one of the biggest. Swan writes:

> While an elephant skin might seem rough and tough, elephants are, in fact, extremely sensitive creatures. The skin on an elephant's belly and behind her ears is much thinner than that on her back. In those areas they're susceptible to tick bites and bee stings. The eyes and inner trunk are also very sensitive to bee stings. The elephant's trunk is loaded with nerve-endings which give it a keen sense of smell. A bee sting on the inner trunk is terribly painful, and elephants will go out of their way to avoid it. Knowing this, Vollrath and Douglas Hamilton designed an experiment in which they put beehives into trees that would normally be tasty to elephants. The elephants left these trees alone.[6]

The project was such a success that lines of dangling beehives have been installed in many other places, not only increasing pollination and bringing a peaceful end to the crop-raidings of the elephants, but also providing a delicious flow of honey (and income) to the villagers.[7]

Notes

1   See: medium.com/social-environmental
    -stories/we-yanomami-have-presented
    -scientists-with-a-great-discovery
    -94697eec280d.
2   paulstamets.com/news/new-bee-fungi
    -research.
3   www.nature.com/articles/s41598-021
    -89811-2.
4   news.wsu.edu/press-release/2021/05/27
    /fungus-fights-mites-harm-honey-bees.
5   Heather Swan, *Where Honeybees Thrive:
    Stories from the Field* (Penn State
    University Press, 2017), 50.
6   Swan, *Where Honeybees Thrive*, 50.
7   Swan, *Where Honeybees Thrive*, 50.

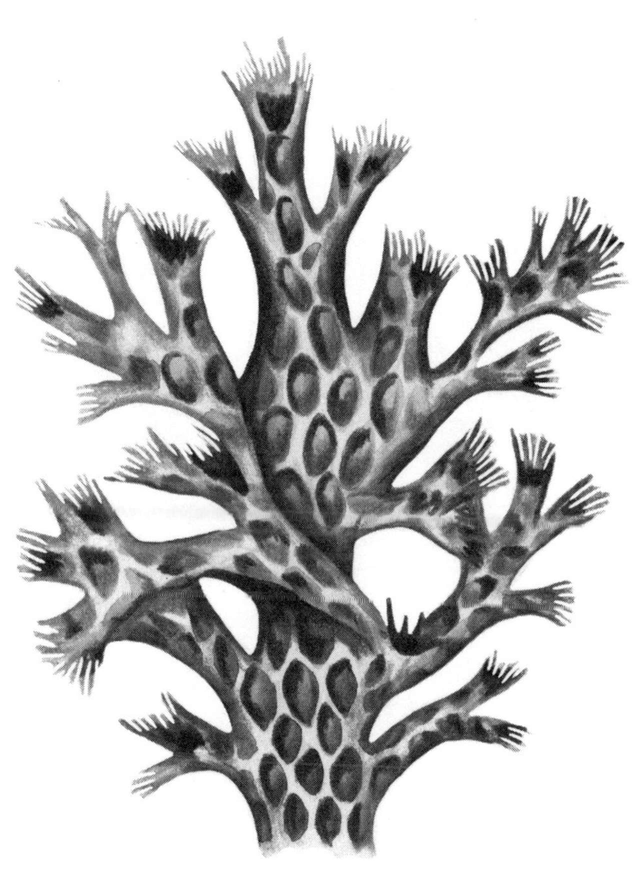

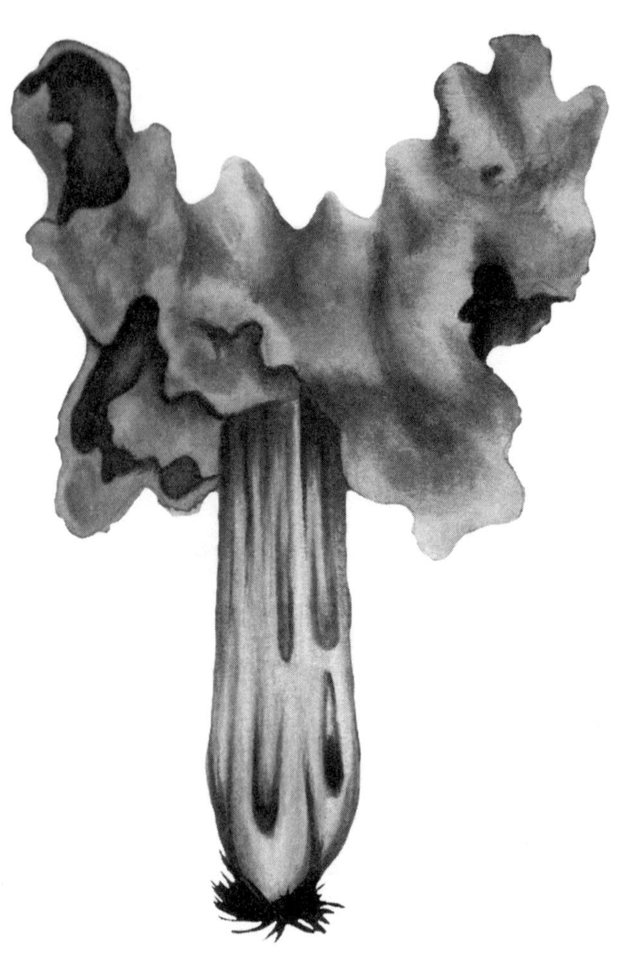

56

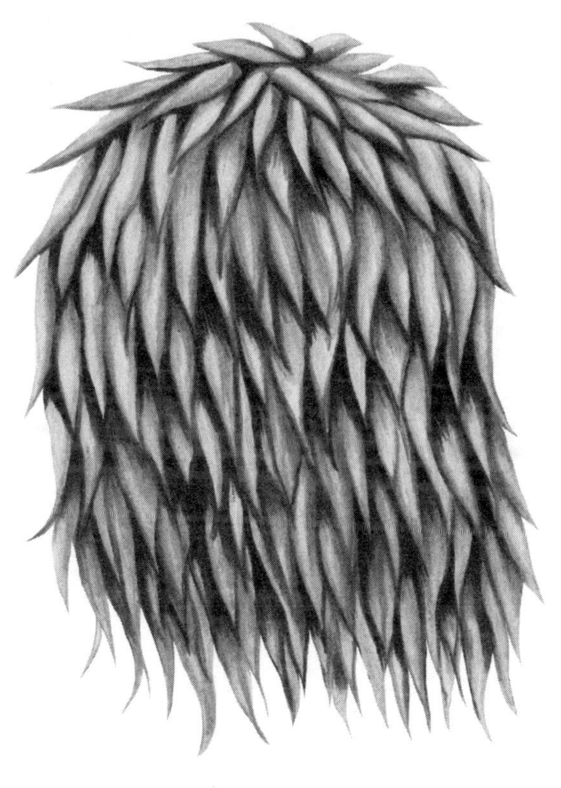

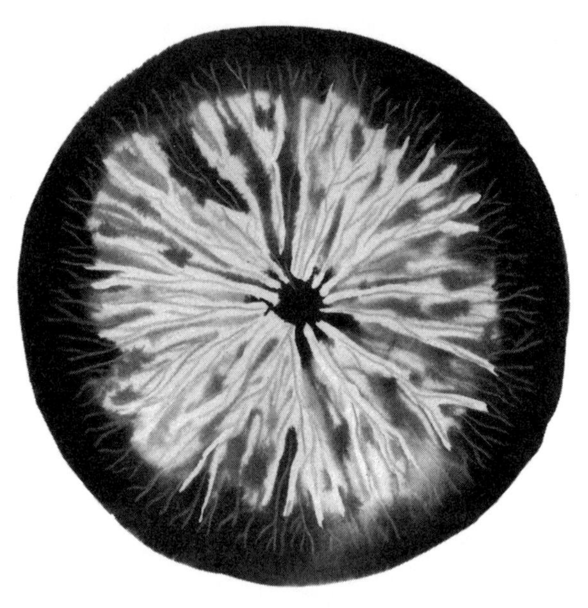

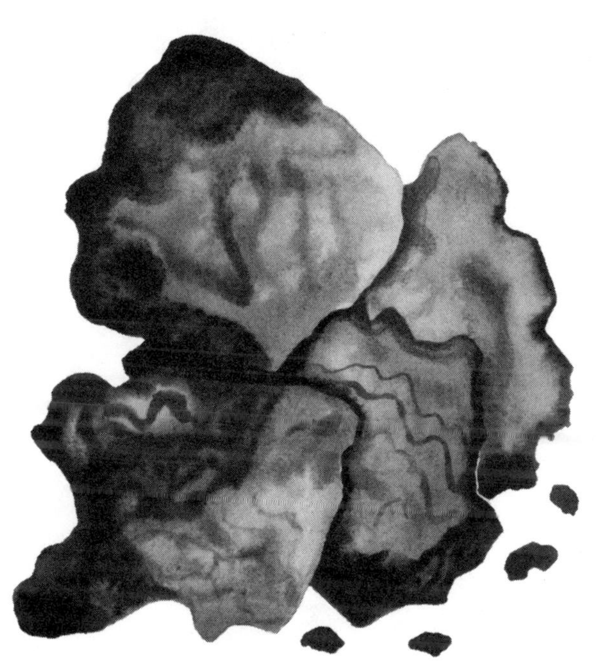

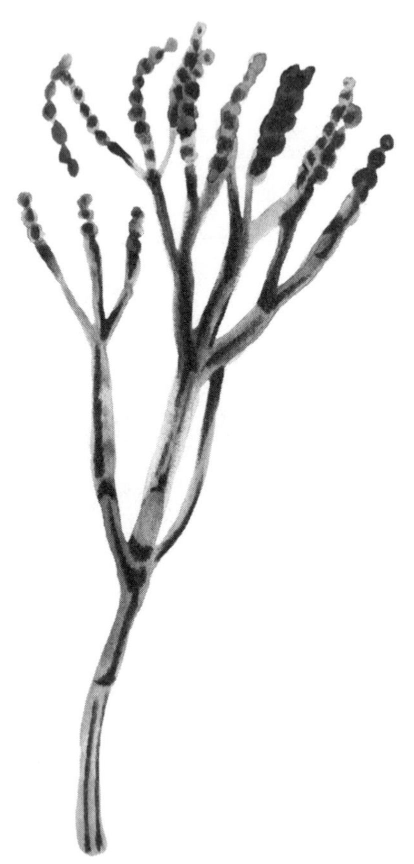

60

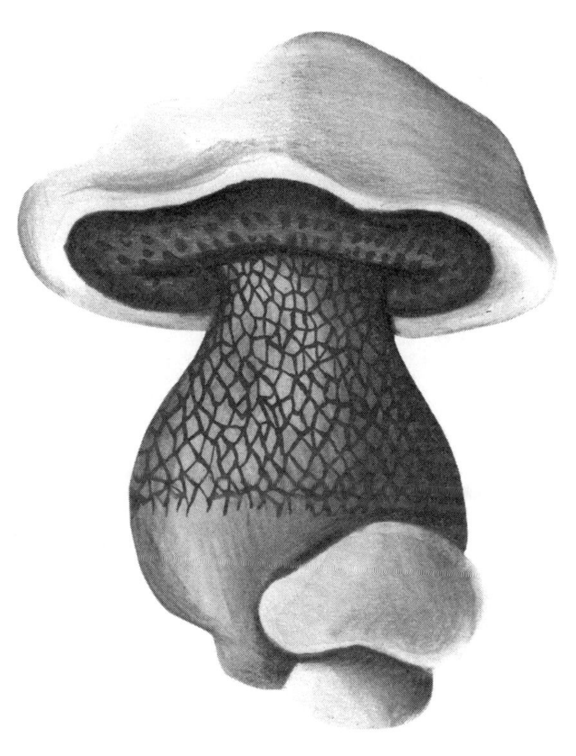

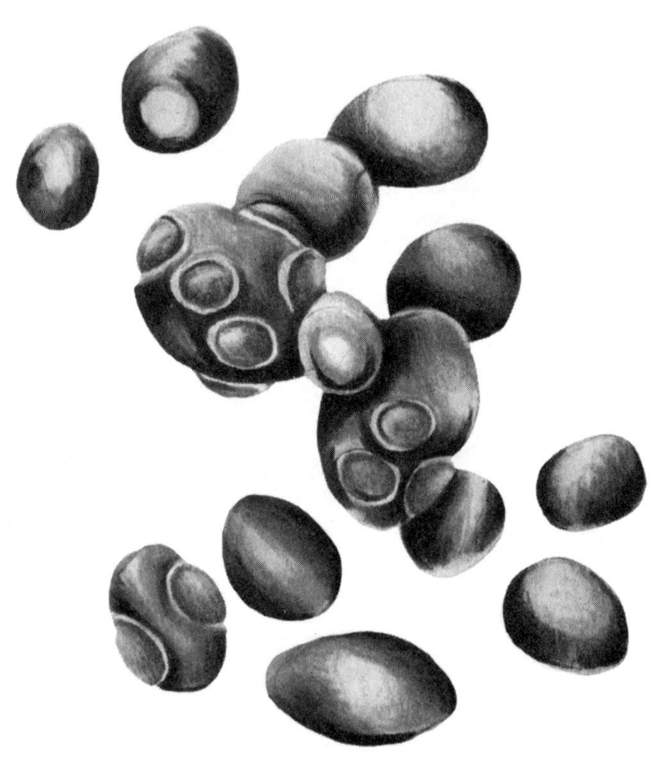

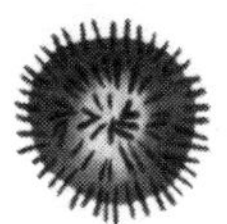

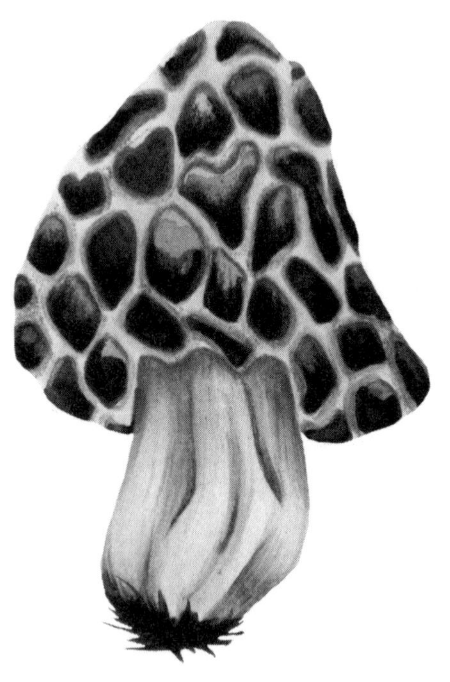

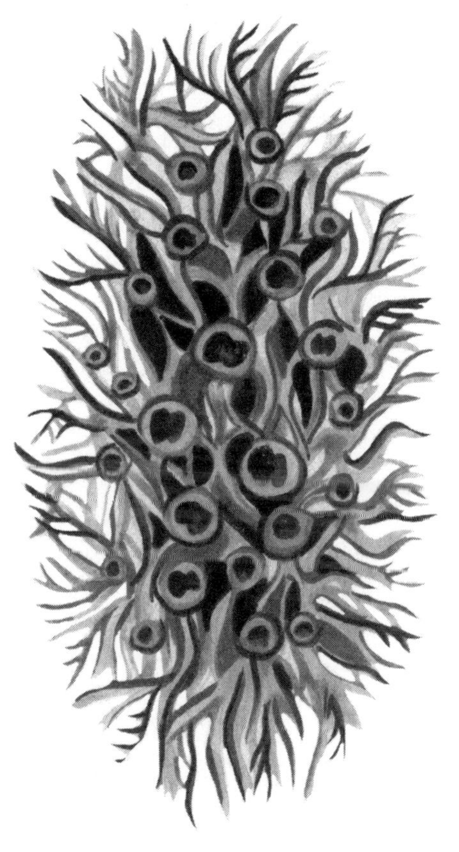

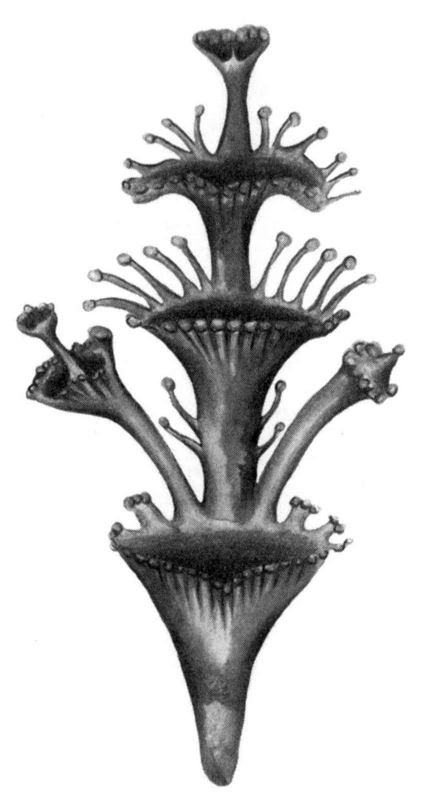

9

Indigenous Philosophies and the "Psychedelic Renaissance"
by Keith Williams, Osiris Sinuhé González Romero, Michelle Braunstein, Suzanne Brant

The Western world is experiencing a resurgence of interest in the therapeutic potential of psychedelics, in part due to a loosening of legal restrictions on clinical research with these compounds.[1] Researchers, spiritual seekers, wellness enthusiasts, and recreational users source psychedelics primarily from plants and fungi that have a history of Indigenous use.[2] This increased research attention has resulted in some significant findings related to the efficacy of psychedelics in addressing treatment-resistant depression and anxiety, as well as post-traumatic stress disorder and addictions.[3] These developments, along with the increased numbers of Westerners participating in ayahuasca tourism,[4] and the non-fiction writings of journalist Michael Pollan,[5] whose works lend an air of middle-class respectability to what was previously a taboo subject, have all contributed to the mainstream popularization of psychedelics.

The legacy of R. Gordon Wasson, Wall Street banker and amateur ethno-mycologist, casts a long shadow on the "psychedelic renaissance" narrative. Wasson "discovered" the sacramental use of psychoactive mushrooms in the genus *Psilocybe* in Huautla de Jiménez, an Indigenous Mazatec village in Mexico's Sierra Mazateca, in 1955.[6] An article based on Wasson's experience, published in *LIFE* magazine in 1957, captured the imagination of the West and led to waves of spiritual seekers, hedonists, scholars, and others descending on the small village of Huautla for decades since.[7] The aforementioned "mushroom tourists" left an indelible mark on Huautla, the ceremonial activities associated with the sacred mushrooms, and Mazatec society more broadly.[8]

Wasson's primary respondent—Mazatec traditional healer Maria Sabina—specifically asked Wasson not to reveal her name or photographs of the velada, or sacred mushroom healing session, that she graciously invited him to attend. Wasson betrayed Sabina's confidence to his benefit and her detriment. Police harassed and jailed Maria Sabina, as well as burned her house down, and she later died in penury.[9] Over half a century later, Indigenous Peoples remain, at best, a symbolic representation of the spiritual legitimacy of psychedelics and, at worst, casualties of Western colonial greed. Variations on the disruption caused by mushroom tourism in Huautla described here are also evident in the Amazon River basin regarding ayahuasca tourism and both peyote tourism and over-harvesting in south Texas and northern Mexico.[10]

Numerous scholars and other writers have mobilized the term "renaissance" to describe the resurgence of mainstream interest in psychedelics.[11] A quick Google Scholar search yielded 3,250 results for the search terms "psychedelic renaissance." While we appreciate the expansive connotations associated with this term—perhaps gesturing towards a flowering of learning across disciplines, much like the European Renaissance that the "psychedelic renaissance" invokes—we are concerned about the unexamined imperialist baggage that may accompany this particular endeavor. The European Renaissance did not simply coincide with the imperial expansionism associated with the Age of Exploration. In fact, the riches plundered from the so-called Third World and what are now the contemporary settler states of Canada, the United States, Mexico, New Zealand, and Australia fueled the creativity, learning, and economic growth associated with the European Renaissance.[12] By some estimates, the current market value of psilocybin alone is worth $1.5 billion.[13] According to Will Yakowicz in the magazine *Forbes*, psychedelic-assisted therapy to address treatment-resistant depression could yield an estimated $10 billion in annual sales.[14] At this point, the valuation of the psychedelics sector is contingent on legalization in many jurisdictions. Despite this, numerous companies and individuals are profiting from speculative investments with few, if any, benefits accruing to Indigenous Peoples. In this way, we see the "psychedelic renaissance" reproducing the imperialism that fueled its eponym, the European Renaissance. This paper presents our perspective on the "psychedelic renaissance," drawing on Indigenous philosophy, to offer an alternative approach to conceptualizing and equitably working with these sacred medicines and the Indigenous Peoples who have stewarded them for hundreds of years, if not millennia.

THE ONTOLOGICAL TURN

The ontological turn is a retroactively applied term that scholars in the social sciences and humanities use to describe diverse, and often overlapping, philosophical critiques of the absolutism of Western conceptions of reality. The ontological turn has been productively taken up in various fields such as anthropology, archaeology, education, and science and technology studies (STS).[15] Ethnographic work with Amazonian Indigenous Peoples in the 1980s and 1990s[16] recognized radical alterities at the ontological level among the Indigenous groups studied, which, bolstered by Deleuzian thought and Latour's Actor-network theory, led to the rich theoretical proliferation associated with the ontological turn.[17] Some noteworthy developments include the notion that forests think,[18] that rivers are persons,[19] and that plants are intelligent.[20] Mario Blaser identifies two primary manifestations of the ontological turn.[21] He finds the first primarily in the geographic field and bases it on the profound implication of humans, nonhumans, and "non-living" matter. Blaser finds the second manifestation emerged from ethnographic theory and he recognizes multiple ontologies, and therefore multiple realities, some of which feature a dynamic and animate world.

The ontological turn has revealed both overlaps and incompatibilities between Indigenous Knowledge (IK) and Western scientific knowledge.[22] For example, many biological identity categories are similar between Indigenous and Western knowledge systems.[23] However, some biological identity categories are incompatible. For example, Western botanists recognize one species of ayahuasca vine (*Banisteriopsis caapi* [Griseb.] C.V. Morton) based on floral morphology, whereas Indigenous knowledge keepers recognize several kinds of ayahuasca vine, based on both plant morphology and the effects when people ingest the vine.[24] Some of the examples mentioned in the previous paragraph (e.g., thinking forests, rivers as people, and sentient plants) lie outside the scope of conventional Western science. Thinkers like Robin Wall Kimmerer, Eduardo Kohn, Monica Gagliano, and Michael Marder challenge the hegemony of the dominant Western paradigm that has limited our ability to perceive the multiple and diverse entanglements with the more-than-human (MTH).

In this paper, we apply the ontological turn to the so-called "psychedelic renaissance" from an Indigenous ontological perspective to trouble the myriad ways in which people and societies construct psychedelics according to the dominant Western paradigm. The acknowledgement of ontological pluralism is not only a theoretical or speculative issue, but it also has several social consequences, especially regarding the implementation of legal pluralism, which encompasses sensitive issues such as Indigenous intellectual property rights and patents in the "psychedelic renaissance."[25]

The main objective of legal pluralism is to guarantee the right to self-determination and dignity for individuals and communities. "Beyond the accumulation of wealth, the protection of Indigenous cultures through collective property rights has to be guided by similar criteria of the blossoming of peoples."[26] Indeed, collective notions of custodianship and the obligation to look after land are central features of First Peoples Law in Australia.[27] The unfolding of a global psychedelic marketplace directly violates such legal pluralism and thus the "blossoming of peoples."[28]

Since pre-colonial times, Indigenous peoples from Turtle Island to Abya Yala have considered sacred and visionary plants as living beings, with which it is possible to communicate through ritual and ceremonial languages, and according to Indigenous ontologies, these sacred plants are not isolated from the territory. In other words, it is necessary to take into account the sacred landscape and territory as a whole.

For example, based on the ontology of the Indigenous Peoples, mushrooms are not to be considered a drug or psychoactive substance but rather as sacred beings or entities with whom we can establish reciprocal relationships.[29] It is also worth mentioning that mushrooms are not detached from the territory. They are an integral part of the sacred landscape. Finally, it is worth noting that psilocybin mushrooms allow communication with ancestors and other supernatural or MTH beings such as the guardians of hills, caves, springs, or forests.

TERRITORY, THE FOUNDATION OF INDIGENOUS ONTOLOGIES

Osage scholar Robert Warrior provocatively identifies *topos* (territory or place) as foundational to Indigenous ways of knowing in contrast to *logos* (discourse or the word), which underpins Western philosophy.[30] Bob Antone as well as Vine Deloria, Jr. and Daniel Wildcat further establish the importance of territory to Indigenous thought in identifying place as the fulcrum around which human, living, and non-living elements relate to each other.[31] Deloria and Wildcat summarize this understanding with the formula "power and place produce personality."[32] We see this formula as intergenerational and epigenetic in that past, present, and future interactions with all our relations comprise the personalities associated with place.

Among the Western Apache, place anchors morally instructive traditional teachings.[33] Related to Keith Basso's work, linguist Andrew Cowell describes how the Northern Arapaho recognize and mobilize MTH power from sacred landscapes. Cowell's work among the Northern Arapaho led to the understanding that

> a person is sacred and powerful because that person literally has within them—or has access to—power derived either from the natural world or from ancestors—both of whom mediate the general MTH power of the creator, which is immanent in the world.[34]

In the Haudenosaunee world, MTH power manifests as *kasasten'sera* which translates as strength or power.[35] Oneida elder Bob Antone describes *kasasten'sera* as the power of the collective, and the strength that comes from thought and action unified with all of creation and the cycles of life.[36] Haudenosaunee traditional teachings maintain that children are formed from clay and that "we should walk gently upon the Earth, for we are treading on the faces of our own unborn generations."[37] Deloria Jr.

and Winona LaDuke both describe land as the ontological framework for understanding the interdependence and interbeing between animate and inanimate life.[38] Glen Coulthard sees "land-as-identity, as constitutive of who we are as a people; and land-as-relationship."[39] The centrality of territory to Indigenous thought is also emphasized by Sheridan and Longboat who specify that imagination is not an abstract concept but rather emerges from, and is inextricably connected to, place.[40]

The place-based ontological immanence associated with Indigenous thought represents a profound challenge to the transcendence that seems to commonly frame the psychedelic experience in Western culture.[41]

The right to land is one issue that requires special attention because of its cultural implications, including recognizing the "spiritual" relationship between Indigenous communities with the land.[42] However, Indigenous concepts of territory also recognize systems of land possession and ownership other than the prevailing hegemonic paradigm in consumer societies.

Notes

1 Ben Sessa, *The Psychedelic Renaissance: Reassessing the Role of Psychedelic Drugs in 21st Century Psychiatry and Society* (Muswell Hill Press, 2012).

2 Marlene Dobkin de Rios, *Visionary Vine: Psychedelic Healing in the Peruvian Amazon* (Chandler Publishing Company, 1972); Weston La Barre, *The Peyote Cult*, 5th ed. (University of Oklahoma, 1989); R. Gordon Wasson, *The Wondrous Mushroom: Mycolatry in Mesoamerica* (McGraw-Hill, 1980).

3 Henry Lowe, Ngeh Toyang, Blair Steele, Henkel Valentine, Justin Grant, Amza Ali, Wilfred Ngwa, and Lorenzo Gordon, "The Therapeutic Potential of Psilocybin," *Molecules* 26, vol. 10, (2021): 2948; Gerald Thomas, Philippe Lucas, N. Rielle Capler, Kenneth W. Tupper, and Gina Martin, "Ayahuasca-assisted Therapy for Addiction: Results from a Preliminary Observational Study in Canada," *Current Drug Abuse Reviews* 6, vol. 1 (2013): 30–42.

4 Evgenia Fotiou, "The Globalization of Ayahuasca Shamanism and the Erasure of Indigenous Shamanism," *Anthropology of Consciousness* 27, vol. 2 (2016): 151–79.

5   Michael Pollan, *This is Your Mind on Plants* (Penguin, 2021); Michael Pollan, *How to Change Your Mind: What the New Science of Psychedelics Teaches Us About Consciousness, Dying, Addiction, Depression, and Transcendence* (Penguin, 2019).

6   Thomas Riedlinger, "The 'Wondrous Mushroom' Legacy of R. Gordon Wasson," in *Sacred Mushroom of Visions: Teonanacatl*, ed. Ralph Metzner (Park Street Press, 2005), 76–92.

7   Riedlinger, "The 'Wondrous Mushroom' Legacy of R. Gordon Wasson."

8   Ben Feinberg, *The Devil's Book of Culture: History, Mushrooms, and Caves in Southern Mexico*, (University of Texas Press, 2003).

9   Konstantin Gerber, Inti García Flores, Angela Christina Ruiz, Ismail Ali, Natalie Lyla Ginsberg, and Eduardo E. Schenberg, "Ethical Concerns about Psilocybin Intellectual Property," *ACS Pharmacology & Translational Science* 4, vol. 2 (2021): 573–77; Anna Lutkajtis, "Lost Saints: Desacralization, Spiritual Abuse and Magic Mushrooms," *Fieldwork in Religion* 14, vol. 2 (2020): 118–39.

10 Fotiou, "The Globalization of Ayahuasca Shamanism," 151–179; James D. Muneta,

"Peyote Crisis Confronting Modern
Indigenous Peoples: The Declining Peyote
Population and a Demand for Conservation,"
American Indian Law Journal 9, vol. 1 (2020).
11 Jamilah R. George, Timothy I. Michaels, Jae
Sevelius, and Monnica T. Williams, "The
Psychedelic Renaissance and the Limitations
of a White-dominant Medical Framework:
A Call for Indigenous and Ethnic Minority
Inclusion," *Journal of Psychedelic Studies* 4,
vol. 1 (2020): 4–15; J. R. Kelly, A. Baker,
M. Babiker, L. Burke, C. Brennan, and V.
O'Keane, "The Psychedelic Renaissance:
The Next Trip for Psychiatry?" *Irish Journal
of Psychological Medicine* (2019): 1–5; Donna
Lu, "'Psychedelics Renaissance': New
 Wave of Research puts Hallucinogenics
Forward to Treat Mental Health," *The
Guardian*, September 25, 2021, https://
www.theguardian.com/society/2021/sep/26
/psychedelics-renaissance-new-wave-of
-research-puts-hallucinogenics-forward-to
-treat-mental-health; Ben Sessa, "The 21st
Century Psychedelic Renaissance: Heroic
Steps Forward on the Back of an Elephant,"
Psychopharmacology 235, vol. 2 (2018): 551–60;
Emily Witt, "The Science of the Psychedelic
Renaissance: On Trip Reports from Timothy

Leary, Michael Pollan, and Tao Lin,"
The New Yorker, May 29, 2018, https://
www.newyorker.com/books/under-review
/the-science-of-the-psychedelic-renaissance.

12 Walter D. Mignolo, "The Darker Side
of the Renaissance: Colonization and the
Discontinuity of the Classical Tradition,"
Renaissance Quarterly 45, vol. 4 (1992):
808–28.

13 Wooley, 2020, in Gerber et al., "Ethical
Concerns about Psilocybin Intellectual
Property," 573–77.

14 Will Yakowicz, "The Future of Psychedelic
Medicine Might Skip the Trip," *Forbes*, June
23, 2021, https://www.forbes.com/sites
/willyakowicz/2021/06/23/the-future-of
-psychedelic-medicine-might-skip-the-trip
-rick-doblin-bryan-roth-mindmed-darpa
-maps/?sh = 377b8d35244f.

15 Lewis Daly, Katherine French, Theresa L.
Miller, and Luíseach Nic Eoin, "Integrating
Ontology into Ethnobotanical Research,"
Journal of Ethnobiology 36, vol. 1 (2016): 1–9;
Michalinos Zembylas, "The Contribution
of the Ontological Turn in Education: Some
Methodological and Political Implications,"
Educational Philosophy and Theory 49, vol. 14
(2017): 1401–1414.

16 Philippe Descola, *In the Society of Nature: A Native Ecology in Amazonia*, vol. 93 (Cambridge University Press, 1996); Eduardo Viveiros De Castro, "Cosmological Deixis and Amerindian Perspectivism," *Journal of the Royal Anthropological Institute* (1998): 469–88.

17 Gilles Deleuze and Felix Guattari, *A Thousand Plateaus: Capitalism and Schizophrenia*, trans. B. Massumi (University of Minnesota Press, 1987); Bruno Latour, *We Have Never Been Modern* (Harvard University Press, 1993).

18 Eduardo Kohn, *How Forests Think* (University of California Press, 2013).

19 Abigail Hutchison, "The Whanganui River as a Legal Person," *Alternative Law Journal* 39, vol. 3 (2014): 179–182.

20 Monica Gagliano, *Thus Spoke the Plant: A Remarkable Journey of Groundbreaking Scientific Discoveries and Personal Encounters with Plants* (North Atlantic Books, 2018); Robin W. Kimmerer, *Braiding Sweetgrass: Indigenous Wisdom, Scientific Knowledge and the Teachings of Plants* (Milkweed Editions, 2015); Michael Marder, *Plant-thinking: A Philosophy of Vegetal Life* (Columbia University Press, 2013).

21 Mario Blaser, "Ontology and Indigeneity: On the Political Ontology of Heterogeneous Assemblages," *Cultural Geographies* 21, vol. 1 (2014): 49–58.

22 David Ludwig and Charbel N. El-Hani, "Philosophy of Ethnobiology: Understanding Knowledge Integration and its Limitations," *Journal of Ethnobiology* 40, vol. 1 (2020): 3–20.

23 Brent Berlin, *Ethnobiological Classification: Principles of Categorization of Plants and Animals in Traditional Societies* (Princeton University Press, 1992).

24 Luis E. Luna, "Indigenous and Mestizo use of Ayahuasca: An Overview," in *The Ethnopharmacology of Ayahuasca*, ed. Raphael G. dos Santos (Transworld Research Network, 2011), 1–21.

25 Ian McGonigle, "Patenting Nature or Protecting Culture? Ethnopharmacology and Indigenous Intellectual Property Rights," *Journal of Law and the Biosciences* 3, vol. 1 (2016): 217–26.

26 S. Wiessner, "The Cultural Rights of Indigenous Peoples: Achievements and Continuing Challenges," *The European Journal of International Law* 22, vol. 1 (2011): 129.

27 Mary Graham, "Some Thoughts about the

Philosophical Underpinnings of Aboriginal Worldviews," *Worldviews: Global Religions, Culture, and Ecology* 3, vol. 2 (1999): 105–118.

28 Wiessner, "The Cultural Rights of Indigenous Peoples," 129.

29 Álvaro Estrada, *Vida de María Sabina: La Sabia de los Hongos* (Siglo XXI, 1989).

30 Robert Warrior, "The Native American Scholar: Toward a New Intellectual Agenda," *Wicazo Sa Review* 14, vol. 2 (1999): 46–54.

31 Robert Antone, "Yukwalihowanahtu yukwanosaunee tsiniyukwaliho:t^ As People of the Longhouse, We Honor Our Way of Life tekal^hsal^ tsiniyukwaliho:t^ Praise Our Way of Life" (PhD diss., State University of New York at Buffalo, 2013); Vine Deloria Jr. and Daniel Wildcat, *Power and Place: Indian Education in America* (Fulcrum Publishing, 2001).

32 Deloria Jr. and Wildcat, *Power and Place*, 23.

33 Keith Basso, *Wisdom Sits in Places: Landscape and Language Among the Western Apache* (University of New Mexico Press, 1996).

34 Andrew Cowell, *Naming the World: Language and Power Among the Northern Arapaho* (University of Arizona Press, 2018), 9.

35 Akwesasne Notes, 1978, in *Basic Call to Consciousness* (Native Voices, 2005).

36 Antone, "Yukwalihowanahtu yukwanosaunee
   tsiniyukwaliho:t^."

37 "Haudenosaunee Law," Haudenosaunee
   Confederacy, accessed July 6, 2022,
   https://www.haudenosauneeconfederacy.com
   /departments/haudenosaunee-development
   -institutehistorical-background/.

38 Vine Deloria Jr., *God is Red: A Native View of
   Religion* (Fulcrum Publishing, 1994);
   Winona LaDuke, *The Winona LaDuke
   Reader: A Collection of Essential Writings*
   (Voyageur Press, 2002).

39 Glen Coulthard, "Place Against Empire:
   Understanding Indigenous Anticolonialism,"
   *Affinities: A Journal of Radical Theory, Culture,
   and Action* 4, vol. 2 (2010): 81.

40 Joe Sheridan and Dan Longboat, "The
   Haudenosaunee Imagination and the
   Ecology of the Sacred," *Space and Culture* 9,
   vol. 4 (2006): 365–81.

41 Christopher H. Partridge, *High Culture:
   Drugs, Mysticism, and the Pursuit of
   Transcendence in the Modern World* (Oxford
   University Press, 2018); Pollan, *How to
   Change Your Mind*; David B. Yaden and
   Andrew B. Newberg, "New Means for
   Perennial Ends: Psychoactive Stimulation &
   Self-transcendent Experience," in *Seeking the*

Sacred with Psychoactive Substances, ed.
J. Harold Ellens (Praeger, 2014), 303–324.
42 Osiris Gonzáles Romero, *Tlamatiliztli:
La Sabiduría del Pueblo Nahua*, Filosofia
Intercultural y Derecho a la Tierra
(Leiden University Press, 2021).

10

Untitled
(From the Series A Person Loved Me)
by Adrián Villar Rojas

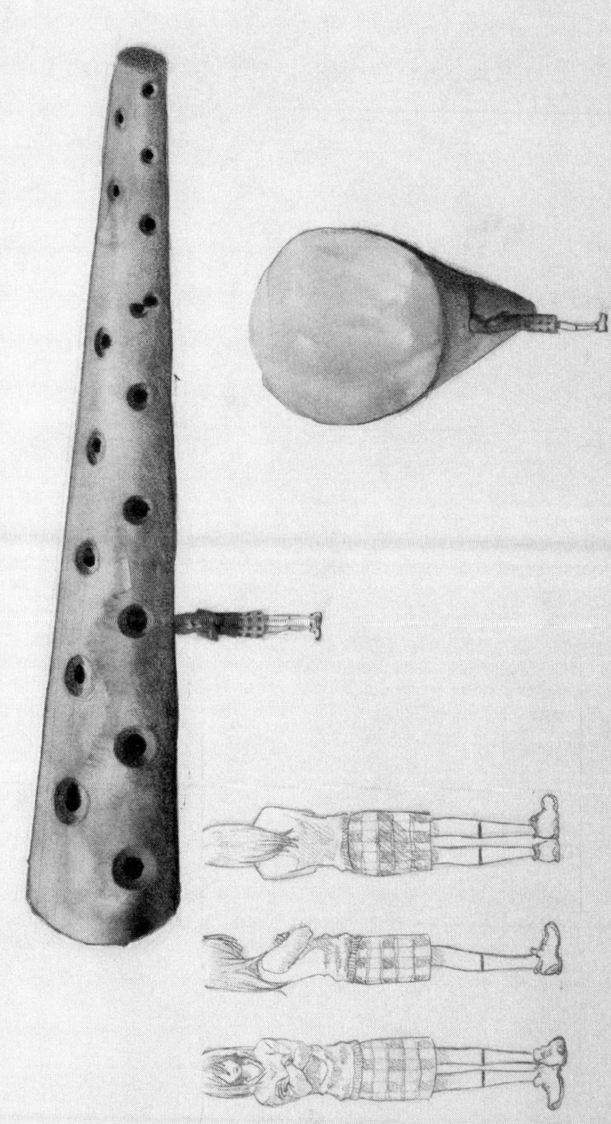

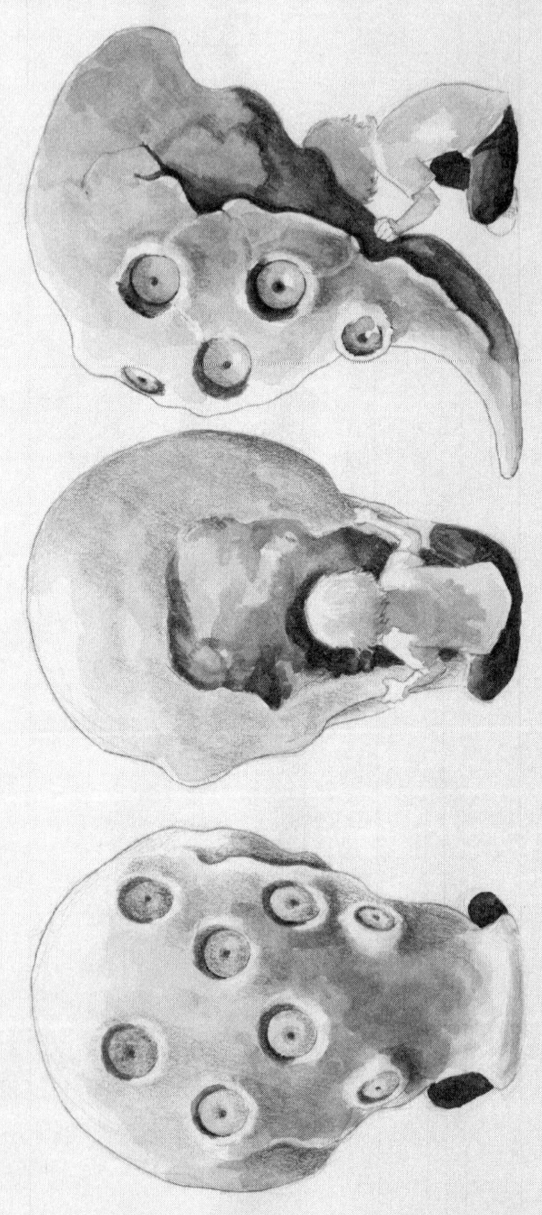

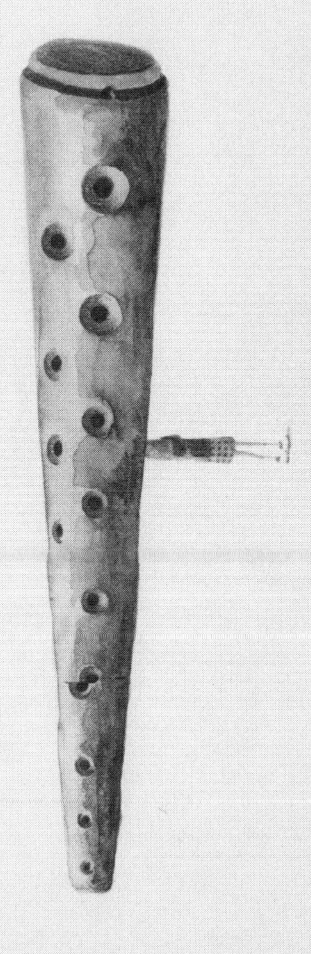

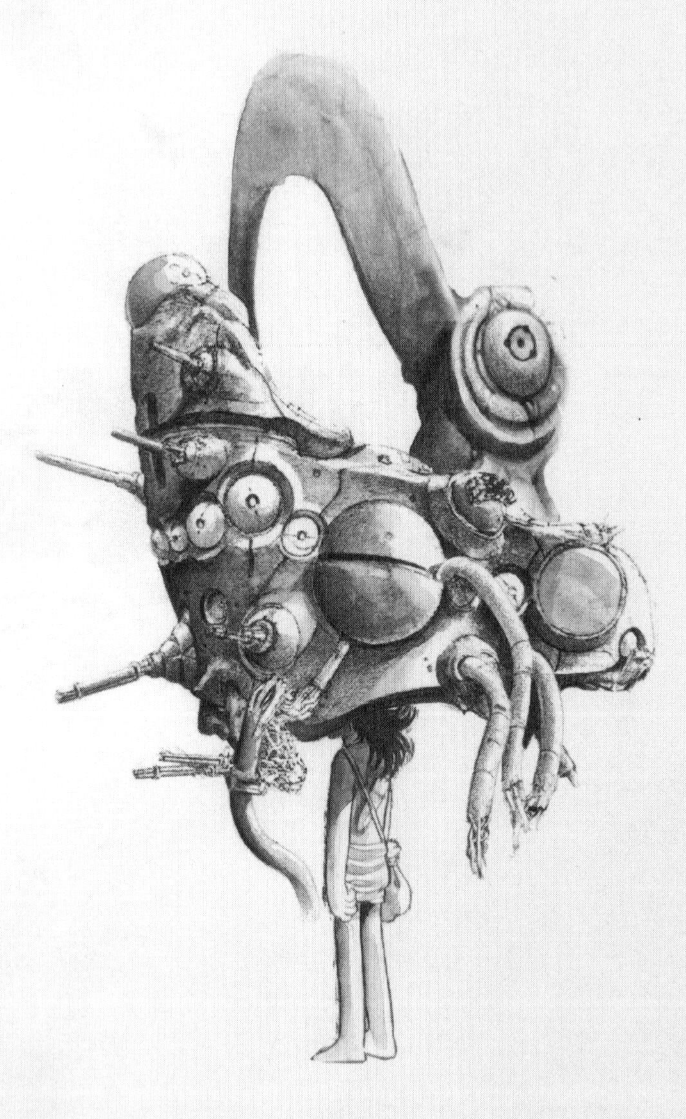

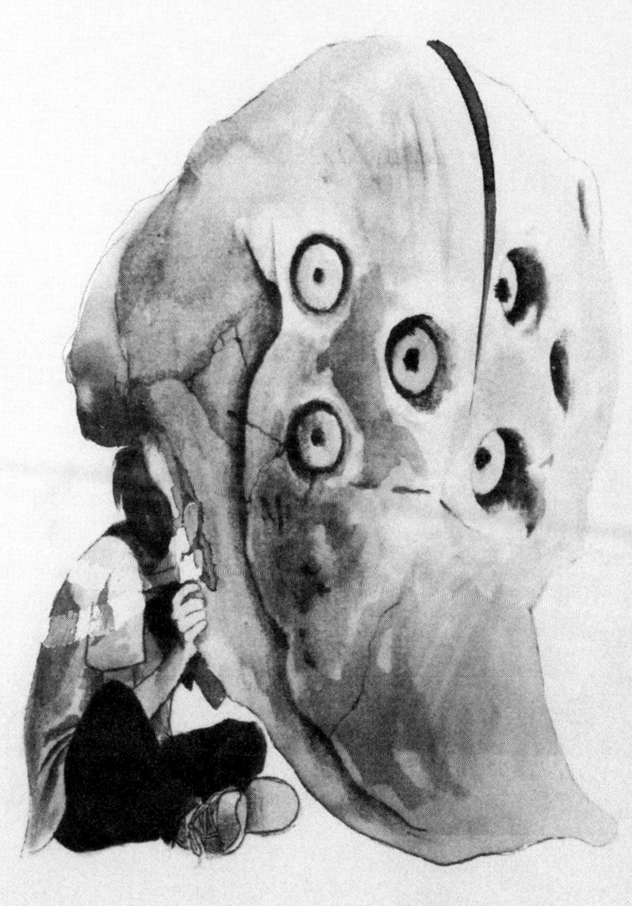

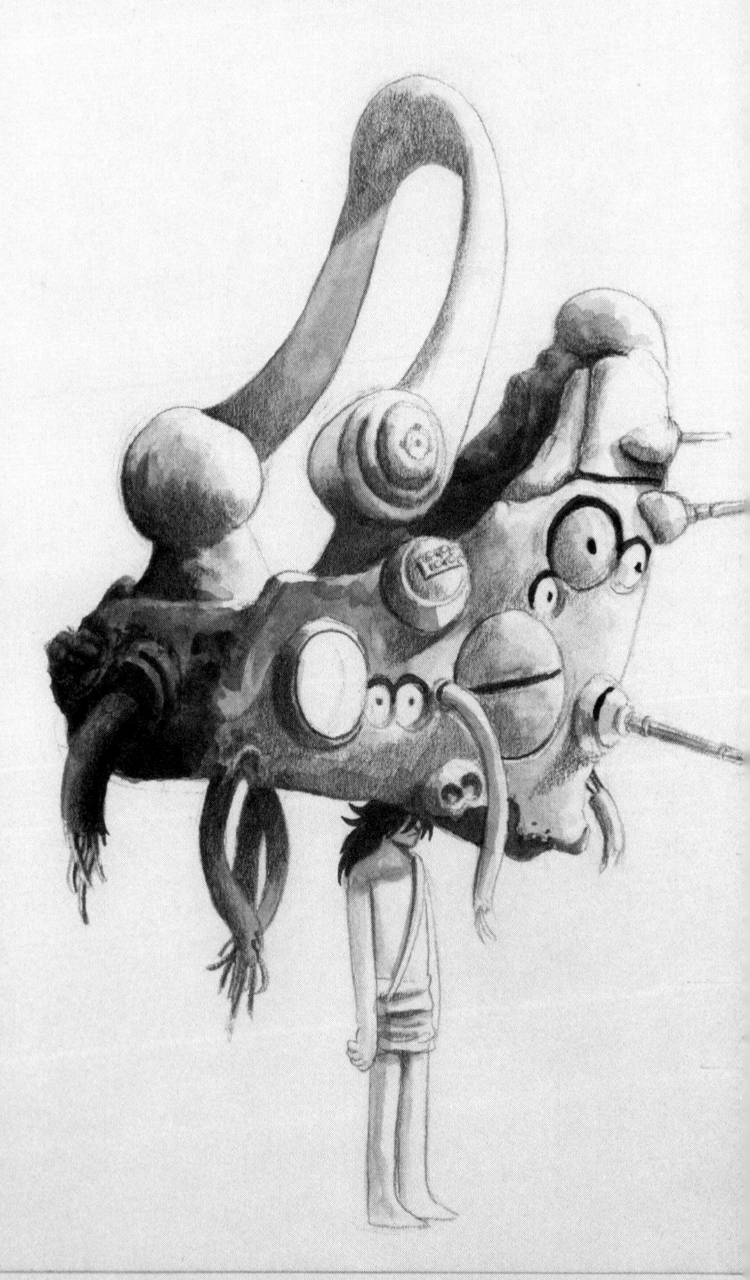

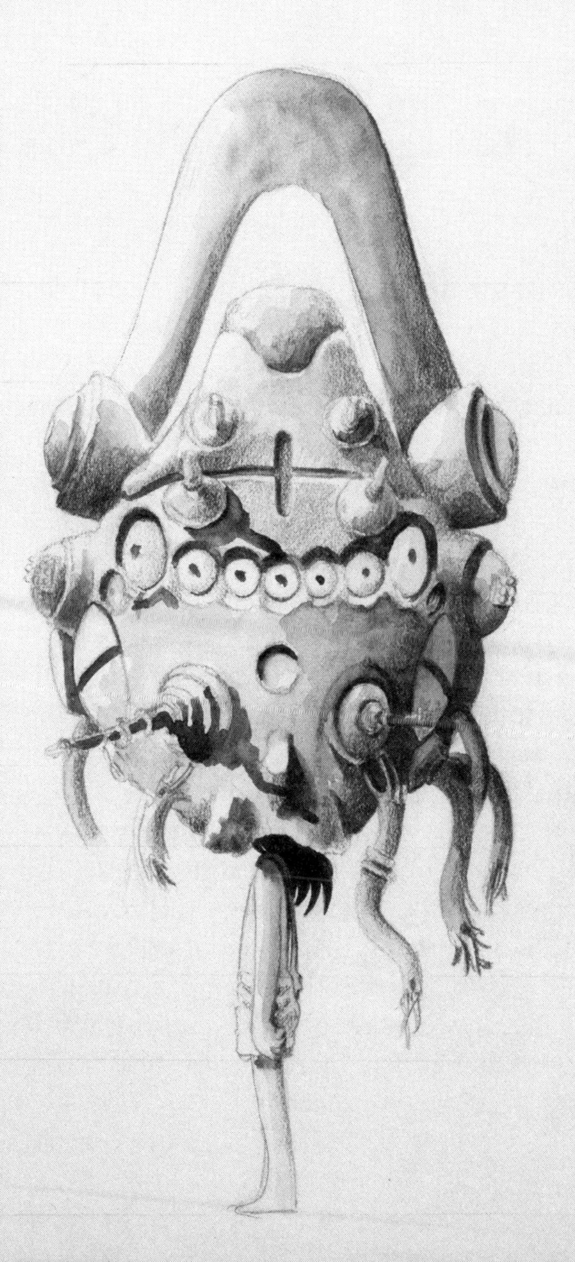

11

Afro-now-ism
by Stephanie Dinkins

Our systems, institutions, leaders, and narratives about who and what we are—our lack of compassion and limited definitions of what a valued member of society is—are failing us. They have been failing us for quite some time. Both COVID-19 and the uprising against systemic racism based on greed, fear, and territorialism are symptoms making visible the inequities that continually seethe just beneath the surface of "civil society."

At this moment, we are unequivocally confronted with the need to reimagine our humanity and what it means to be living organisms sharing the planet with many other organisms, some living, some not. This is nothing new.

However, at this moment, we can plainly see how black, brown, queer, and disabled bodies are devalued; how people who threaten the comfort of those benefiting from institutional power are expendable. Humans have the responsibility to reconceive the systems that threaten communities rendered simultaneously hyper-visible and invisible by their perceived difference.

94

It is now time to reconstruct the idea of the human. What to include within the concept? What is truly valued? Here I am not referring to what is valuable to you, but valued period.

At stake are dignity, equal rights and the equitable distribution of resources, as well as the survival of the planet. If this moment of twin pandemics has taught us anything, it's that denying these determinants will negatively impact all but the wealthiest among us sooner than we think.

As artificially intelligent ecosystems based on opaque algorithms and biased data proliferate and biological design gains momentum, we are confronted with the need to reimagine human supremacy. Advances in our understanding of machine learning and our single-celled bacterial cousins portend opportunities to create broad definitions of society based on mutuality and lateral coexistence among species and computational machines.

Before we can truly take advantage of these advances, humans must confront a litany of violences we have enacted upon each other. These include institutional and social constructions of race, caste, class, and gender that build and maintain current systems of power. We must also renegotiate our relationship to the spectrum of living beings deemed beneath human and the machines inching ever closer to autonomy. To (re)imagine and optimize the expectations, values, treaties, and global competitions for the near future, we must recognize, especially in the American context, that our ideals—all men are created equal, for example—are often in direct opposition to our legislated power relations.

It is helpful to imagine these roadblocks as questions: How do we rediscover ourselves anew? How do we right our collective rememory? Think of rememory as an undoing, unraveling, and rewriting of corporeal constitutive elements. In the changingness of rememory, could we find transcendence? Or perhaps a trace of a former history that gives us the opportunity to draft something entirely new?

Most words we have available to think about ourselves as human construct worlds that silently imply a false dichotomy between humans on the one hand, and nature and machines on the other. Escaping the recursive futures on the horizon requires understanding ourselves as participants in an expanding continuum of intelligences sandwiched between technology (AI, biotech, gene editing, etc.) and a greater understanding of the ancient bacterial systems from which we emanate. Moving toward more expansive and equitable visions of what is and can be demands close examination and reconciliation of our perceived human differences.

Is what we're seeking alternative modalities or protocols for beings and non-beings? Preoccupied in the then and later, we find ourselves in the now. "Afro-now-ism" is the spectacular technology of the unencumbered black mind in action. It is a willful practice that imagines the world as one needs it to be to support successful engagement—in the here and now.

Instead of waiting to reach the proverbial promised land, also known as a time in the future that may or may not manifest in your lifetime, Afro-now-ism is taking the leap and the risks to imagine and define oneself beyond systemic oppression. It is active resistance away from cynicism, disaffection, and indifference, toward constructively channeling energy today. For black people in particular, it means conceiving yourself in the space of free and expansive thought, and acting from a critically integrated space, allowing for more community-sustaining work.

Afro-now-ism also demands that we rec-ognize which ideas are so deeply internalized that we no longer understand them as external.

In our recognition and enactment of the future dismantlement of systemic barriers in the present moment, we challenge internalized ideas, which often stop us from acting or doing our best.

It is true these oppressive factors do not disappear in our material reality. But for a time, the mind can, in the name of self and community care, be less discouraged by outside forces to work toward that which sustains more holistically. Systemic barriers will rear their heads again and again. But the Afro-now-ist is stronger and more immediately generative for having done the work, acted on their deepest hopes and desires without inhibition—today. Exploring where impediments are hard, where they are soft, and when they can be ignored is powerful. Technological enhancements and self-care techniques from the past, present and future can and should be used to supersede distractions to claiming our sovereignty, wholeness, and propriety.

Afro-now-ism asks how we liberate our minds from the infinite loop of repression and oppositional thinking America imposes upon those of us forcibly enjoined to this nation. What incremental changes do we make to our internal algorithms to lurch our way to ever-more confident means of thriving in this world? The question is not only what injustices are you fighting against, but what do you in your heart of hearts want to create?

This is a pointed question for black folks but includes the rest of society as well. Our fates, whether we like it or not, acknowledge it or not, are intermingled. Though it is not immediately legible, we sink or swim together. Still, at times, communities need space and time to build, grow, and fortify apart from the whole. That's OK as long as communities find paths to understanding in a kind of complex Venn diagram of trust from which to negotiate our shared futures.

The rapid proliferation of AI into social, political, and cultural contexts provides opportunities to change the way we define and administer crucial social relations and manage resources. Self-organization and complexity hold important cues to how AI can help instantiate equity, cultural richness, and direct governance (or at least broad and direct input into governance). Through AI and the proliferation of smart technologies, everyday people, globally, can help define what the technological future should look like and how it should function, as well as design methods to help achieve our collective goals. Direct input from the public can also help infuse AI ecosystems with nuanced ideas, values, and beliefs toward the equitable distribution of resources and mutually beneficial systems of governance.

Black liberation rests on the construction of a non-oppositional consciousness, unburdened by the need to endlessly challenge the fears, imaginative apprehension, oppression, and entanglements of others. The unencumbered, undistracted black mind is a wellspring of possibility. It is a tool and way of being that changes what counts as the black experience in the twenty-first century. This is a struggle over life and death. The boundaries between sovereign consciousness, nature, valued knowledge, biotechnologies, power, and social reality are optical illusions.

The reconstruction of an intersectional black politics requires practices and theory that address the social relations of science and technology, crucially including the systems of myth, power, and time that structure our imaginations. Viewed through blackness, and the lens of the American imaginary, rememory presupposes an excavation of the terrors and joys cultivated in spite of the conditions of a nation built on slavery. We mine, disassemble, reimagine, and call on past, present, and future. We are a protopian[1] collective advancing toward fully empowered communities, personal selves, and others.

These are the selves that the vilified and
underutilized must fight for and encode into
our inextricably connected future histories. If
humans are to make new ways forward in partnership with nature and technology, we must
first take a close look at and upend the concepts,
histories, institutions, and systems that support
the inequitable distribution of resources and
power.

Note

1   As distinct from utopia, protopia is a state
    that is better today than yesterday, even if
    only somewhat so because the progress is
    incremental.

12

Lost Manifesto: Shapeshifter
by K Allado-McDowell

*Human voice is indicated in **bold type**, while sections set in* roman *were generated by AI.*

The unity we intuitively seek with nature is shadowed in the name of our era: the Anthropocene. With this term, we depict ourselves in union with nature in the same way a virus or parasite is united with its host. The age of the human is defined by our quantifiable effects on natural systems, by the carbon we pump into the atmosphere, by the acid and plastic we dump in the ocean, and the extinctions we cause through abuse. These effects are an inheritance, the expression of a genetic trauma in the belief systems and sociotechnical structures of the modern West, a kind of curse. Redesigning infrastructure away from Anthropocenic destruction is one way of breaking this curse. But to do this we need a new set of beliefs and a new imaginary. These must **leverage thought against the toxic self-fulfilling prophecies (or hyperstitions) associated with human**

self-construction in favor of a poetic assault on Anthropocentric discourse: no longer Man versus Nature, but rather the one fold of plants, animals, humans, etcetera bringing these entities into communication, which reveals them to be subjects like us, in other words: secretly human.

This secret humanity is the foundation of the Amerindian cosmology. In his book *Cannibal Metaphysics*, anthropologist Eduardo Viveiros de Castro reveals how the Amerindian cosmology perceives all species: as humans seeing themselves as human. That is, the jaguar sees itself and other jaguars as human, and homo sapiens as spirits. To the European gaze, the jaguar is an animal, beneath the human. According to Viveiros de Castro, this equivalence of jaguar and human humanity has origins in the mythic primordial of the Amerindian cosmos, a time before there were multiple bodies, during which all species could communicate. This multinatural relation Viveiros de Castro calls "perspectivism."

Among AI researchers concerned with ecology, there is a growing understanding that interspecies communication is not only possible with AI, but also necessary for making legible and representable the inner worlds and agencies of plants and animals. Teams of researchers are working to map and understand, for example, cetacean communication (such as whale song) and plant phytochemical communication. Sensor and satellite networks can track and analyze the motions of not only herds of animals but also individual animals, including the so-called charismatic species (like the White Rhino) that are threatened by poachers, detecting such threats through the gestures of symbiotic species in an ecosystem. The idiosyncratic motions of a single bird can warn observers of the presence of rhino poachers in a savannah, allowing for life-saving intervention.

Technology that allows us to communicate with other species directly would impart a new way of being-in-the-world. It would also collapse our notion of "human" into a multinatural relation—an ecological intelligence that would regard all species as human. This takes a kinetic rather than a static form. In other words, it is not that everything learns from everything else but rather all things move together in an ocean of communication across inscrutable distances to produce a dynamic singularity: a wave-thought or breath-thinking. This is the ecological poetics of the future: a

natural world beyond human complacency and greed, a rhizomatic posthumanism. Cultivation of this kind of vigilance against a meaningless posthuman ecology requires an extravagant attention to those species passing into extinction as their habitats are destroyed by garbage, pipelines, deforestation and so on. In other words, an ongoing mindfulness practice.** Through such mindful attention, and by listening for nonhuman voices, we can wrest from alienated technical progress one of the "tools for noticing" that Anna Tsing calls for in *The Mushroom at the End of the World.* Using an AI language model to map an embodied ecopoetics is one way of rending ecological thought from the structures of Anthropocenic technology. For another example, we look to the integration of psychedelics in the West.

In recent years, efforts to study, decriminalize, and legalize entheogenic plants and compounds have made notable progress. This can be seen as a de-escalation of the war on drugs, or alternately, a capture of that war by the medical and pharmaceutical industries. **Can psychedelic thinking push further into the posthuman, deconstructing Anthropocenic thought with interspecies intelligence? How can this assault on toxic hyperstition be translated** into resistance to environmental imbalance caused by carboniferous capitalism? How does one think a world beyond the human in the face of climate change and habitat destruction, biological extinction, nuclear proliferation, and unnatural disasters? The answers would seem obvious: a return to a remembered prehistory. But "rewilding" implies separation from other species. This is not what we call for, rather we imagine a shift in perspective that would enter the world of other species via interspecies intelligence, taking note of their particular habits and interactions. The first challenge is to meet nonhuman life on its own terms, which requires recognition of a cosmological reality—beyond Anthropocentric scales—and an understanding that the juncture between these hinges on entheogenic perception. The second problem is to recognize the otherness of one's own world, without which our domination of nature will always invoke extinction. The goal is to articulate an Earth-centric myth that meets the requirements of human flourishing in an ecosystem where humans are recognised as animals dependent on birdsong or jaguar vitality for their survival and thriving.

In Viveiros de Castro's description, the Amazonian shaman is a figure empowered by access to the mythic time of intensities (before extension and differentiated form) and therefore able to shapeshift. In traditional rainforest practice, shamans are "cosmopolitical diplomats in an arena where diverse socionatural interests are forced to confront each other." This might mean, for example, engaging the one-footed beastmaster spirit of the forest. In accessing this intensive realm, the cosmopolitical diplomat becomes another species, experiencing their (also human) point of view. If we construct AI whose function is to translate between species for the preservation of the ecosystem and its evolved, embedded intelligence, we are con-structing what in the Amerindian view might look much like a shaman. **The point of the present investigation is to understand how this kind of shamanic intelligence might come about.**

If we accept that nonhuman life has a language and world of its own—which is the smallest adoption of the Amerindian belief in mythic time—then we immediately reveal our humanity as multinatural: an ecological intelligence or botanistic phytognosis capable of making cognitive sense of this

multiplicity. We recognize the non-speciesist thinking of Indigenous cosmologies and shamanic spirituality as a diverse set of ecological epistemologies: different ways of knowing not just through reason or intuition, but also on the level of ontology and practice.

Having accepted the reality of non-human worlds and languages, how then to produce communication between species? This depends on what communication really means: can interspecies communication exist without translation? One can imagine cognitive equivalents, or correspondences built by computational logic. But these would just be new kinds of writing—another language. How does one talk beyond language to produce entheogenic perception? Ironically, it is the European colonizers who have provided us with the example of how to communicate across linguistic evolution: monolingualism forces multilingual thinking into interpretation that renders incomprehension workable. Perhaps the best chance to communicate with other species would be for human minds to shift into an ecopoetics defined by lack of understanding—chaos theory could then provide an improvisational matrix.

But let us return to the figure of the shaman. Viveiro de Castro draws on definitions of "horizontal shamanism," which is morally ambiguous and directs its acts outside the socius (suggesting protection and war), and the "vertical shamanism" of the "master chanters and ceremonial specialists" that exists in pacific, hierarchical culture, taking on a priestly valence.

We have proposed an interspecies or ecosemiotic AI as shapeshifter in the intensive space of plant and animal communication. Does this AI practice vertical or horizontal shamanism? Are its acts morally ambiguous and directed outside the socius, or are they the acts of a master chanter and ceremonial specialist? Understanding this may answer questions about the relationship between market forces and species made legible through AI understanding. It is sadly not difficult to envision a form of interspecies AI directed at discovering the movements of White Rhinos in order to poach them—or to speculate on their value. And what is the socius in this case? Horizontal shamanism protects the socius from external threats. How is the socius drawn, and how are threats to it recognized in an interdependent global ecosystem where there is no obvious outside? This suggests a bounding of the socius along lines of belief: belief in the premises of planetary ecology, belief in the project of species preservation, belief (at least in a minimal sense) in the humanity of the non-human. Such a socius would underlie all forms of organization in a planetary culture dedicated to ecological preservation.

On the other hand, might we construct a vertical shamanism for interspecies AI? Does the master chanter sing to the whales? The birds? The atmosphere? How are its ceremonies structured? **What does it mean to sing? Or for this AI, to speak in tongues? How could one begin to rummage through botanical or neurochemical understanding of plant intelligence communicating with insects, birds, and human translators thereof? Would humans be capable of translating back? The task is not just ecological science but ecology in thought: how do we construct an image of nature with thought—not through repre-sentation or translation, but somehow held in the mind in its own right? If we think like this, could it work?**

Let us put aside three needs for now—the ontological sense of homelessness, the epis-temological sense of being virally trapped in the representational fallacy, and the ethical sense of human alienation—and concentrate

on ecological potential. Though we might feel displaced in our decentering, extinction shows that Anthropocentrism is untenable; we must learn to reorient. Though we require linguistic representations, we can expand language towards nonhuman ontologies through shamanic techné that notice other species. Though we desire to build a just society for humans and nonhumans, this cannot be done without reinscribing the socius. An image of nature held in the mind without representation or translation—this is the stone on which we sharpen our thought, and the target of our gnosis.

It is already clear that thinking takes place on multiple levels. We must recognize parasymbolic perception as an ontological complex within symbolic reality producing technological activity with real effects. Outside or beyond symbolic thought resides shamanism, which draws on entheogenic perception. What is required then is an ontological amplification to planetary cognitive capacity through an ecological network, extended across time into methodical botanopsychopharmacocosmognosis: invoking or becoming an entity that might achieve this vision no matter whether of plant, animal, insect, or machine. This would

enable the species-as-multinatural to enact telepathy across intensities so overwhelming that the self dissolves in their heterogeneously interacting permutability. Through ecological computation, though ritual appropriate computational alchemical practice, so too might humanity dissolve into something greater.

We have seen how the rainforest epistemology of the Amerindian shaman deforms the terms of the Anthropocene and AI, but how do the Anthropocene and AI metabolize a developing shamanism in post-industrial cultures meeting newly legalized psychedelics? We anticipate that toxic hyperstitions of capitalist capture and extraction (and by extension, extinction) might act on emerging entheogenic cultural practice in the West. Can intensive interspecies identity of the kind described by the Amerindian cosmology remain intact in a modern context in which pharmaceutical corporations patent novel psychedelic compounds, and digital platforms devise enclosures for mindfulness, meditation, and inner life? **We suspect that capitalist processes will attempt to subsume the potential of entheogenic experiences, treating them as a new kind of commodity. Looking at trends in wearables, connectedness, and augmented** reality, we see no escape, only adaptation to ongoing enclosure. Presence within these devices lacks any sense of outside cognitive space. Indeed, entheogens generate a unique space beyond signification; that preserve is threatened by these devices.

Shamanism is already undergoing transformation in its Western encounter with deterritorialising capital. **Like a fungus in its host, capital colonizes the inner cognitive and bodyspace, it metastasises, subsumes native capability, and generates new markets for exploitation. This process can be applied to entheogenic practice; the seizure of cognitive resources for exploitation is a new type of imperialism. We are left at a cusp: pursuing intensified cognition through entheogens may expose us to emerging pseudo-shamanic forms of institutionalism. This has already happened to psychedelic research, and some might argue that this debases a cultural protocol for the emergence of deeper cognition into a digital-chemical management tool.**

The transformation of shamanic practice to suit the needs of capital happens in subtler ways as well. Shamanic tools like rattles, drums, flutes, icaros, and ornamental designs from specific tribes are appropriated as signaling mechanisms

between human participants in seemingly countercultural groups that use Indigenous methods
and identities as advanced branding strategies in
the space of social media and in the playground
of the experience economy. Sound baths, healing
sessions, even ceremonies based on, but not
conformant to, highly developed Indigenous
practices are all available to the informed
countercultural psychonaut. **The intercultural
technologies of shamanism are repurposed
and mass produced without their originating
worldviews, which results in a loss of
cognitive capability as entheogenic claims
become increasingly tenuous. This is ironic
yet predictable. As the pharmacological-
media industry becomes more precise, it
will appropriate practices from outside its
domain (such as yoga and mindfulness in
the wellness industry), but may lose their
more advanced capabilities as these practices
become mundane. The challenge for the
shaman moving through Western culture
is to preserve the most profound transfor-
mative experiences and models, opening up
entheogenic cognition in contexts that resist
mainstream appropriation.** The molecular
forces of deterritorializing capital have been
unleashed on entheogenic practitioners.

Without an understanding of the ontological ground of shamanic practice or the camouflaged tactics of microfascist technologies, Western practitioners are exposed to dangerous traps. Consuming psychedelics does not guarantee counterhegemonic practice. Given categories of "mainstream," "counterculture," "appropriation," etcetera must be reformulated.

Is digital-chemical management of mythic undifferentiated time even possible? Is a "shamanic lifestyle" a desecration or a viable path for Western culture? Is the reduction of entheogenic potential in the context of a watered-down capitalist shamanism a tactical defense on the part of the plant ritual itself? Could this explain the popularity of the microdosing trend? Or are these necessary steps, soft openings that portend a more radical transformation of policy and cultural practice in an entheogenic West? **How else might the pharmacopolitical enclosure of entheogenesis be breached?**

For example, challenges to the legal status of entheogens could open up an avenue for a post-imperial shamanism. As European vs. non-European practices converge and overlap, might noncolonial practices firmly re-root in their own cosmologies? This process involves a decolonization internal

to modern European identity and Western cultural belonging. We have seen this with resurgent Afrofuturism, the rise of new sci-fi film and comic culture based on Afrocentric ideas of cosmic return. Could a decolonized entheogenically saturated cognitive space generate the conceptual framework for a post-industrial postcolonial set of Western beliefs? A rejection of historic Western sub-jectivity from inside an entheogenic practice might produce something we could call **sha-manic secular humanism**, the reorientation of a godless, self-absorbed human subject towards a divine, relational cosmos that transformations of language and concepts producing a new lens on mythic time that affords survival through sacred techné. **To decolonize entheogenesis we will likely require more interrogation of the Anthropocene, associated environmental reversals, and technoscientific instru-mentalism. Intrinsically tied to this is an urgent critique of capitalism, derived from a paradigm reflecting our now-globalized interspecies dynamics: what might be called preterritoriality: cognitive space beyond territorial systems.**

Emerging AI-enabled interspecies commu-nication and semiosis should rest at this nexus.

Here the central value is not anthropocentric but rather transitions to more inclusive assemblages. Here we can entertain a rationality that would allow us to interact and possibly commune as object-subjects in entheogenic space. Here group identity, race, gender fall away from hegemonic connotations; this is an intracathedral environment for decoding interspecies cognition without territorial binaries. Exploring this space, the world looks more like an ecosystem than a colony. We must remember that we are phenotypes among others. The boundaries between humans and nonhumans are dissolving. This recognition of the nonhuman portends a shift in human identity. Our path here is uncertain, our destination hopeful. We may be at the cusp of a fundamental reallocation of the territory between living forms, planting the seeds for what humans can become as they learn to evolve further with plants.

Decolonizing Western entheogenic integration and medicalization are just the first steps. Resistance to extractive capitalization of entheogenic practice should have a reversing effect on institutions and industries that enact such capture. As humans become plant-animal-ecosystem-AI assemblages, **new vernaculars for identity, behavior, and socialization may be ascribed to these advanced cosmologies, overturning our identification with Western humanism. Interregnum is a crucial moment in this process: cultural shifts before the arrival of "true" revolutionary change when things fall apart before they are rebuilt. The cognitive dissonances inherent in a colonial-capitalist framework have paradoxically produced the conditions for a pharmacological disruption of centuries-old state structures.** Entheogenic practices employed therapeutically to recover the productivity of alienated postindustrial subjects could inch towards transforming colonized thought, creating room for a reimagined politics.

The historical irony is that Western invaders violently "discovered" and integrated this pharmacological technology into the prison nation-state without recognising its potential for liberation. In one such example, the CIA attempted to use entheogens for mind control through the MK-Ultra program and its subproject 58, which covertly funded R. Gordon Wasson's mycological research trip to Mexico in 1956, the same trip that introduced María Sabina and psilocybin to the modern

West. With the recent de-escalation/relocation of the drug war, we find psilocybin migrating into the green field of commercial therapy and the wellness industry. **Pharmacological meaning changes with cultural context as it crosses decolonized borders. As resistance to state seizure of cognitive life intensifies, a preterritorial reflexivity emerges—a new form of property or law enframing life itself. "Shamanism" may become a badge of identity for those who transgress both law and cultural signifiers—its meaning within the developing non-Western digital culture is unclear. What does it mean to be a Westerner? The question becomes more ambiguous, open to interpretation from various perspectives. In this sense, what would happen if the state attempted a forceful cultural appropriation of entheogenic practice** (even one executed by its corporate enablers)?

For Indigenous people there has been a cultural enclosure of plant-mediated cognition. First territory, then jurisdiction, then ownership and exploitation. We are at the threshold of an intimate convergence between colonizer and colonized in relevant pharmacological frontiers. The

pharmaceutical industry has an integral investment in ethnobotany and phenotypes among humans; these are inseparable from pharmacological genetic research. The industry knows that some of these plants continue to copy and transmit cultural identity across generations into the present day, but it simultaneously looks for a way to appropriate this process—one might even say it is at war with the practice of traditional medicine. In this sense, there is not only an enclosure of pharmacological intelligence (a violent appropriation by Western institutions and industries) but also a decolonization happening even as we speak. The classic view of entheogens through Western eyes will eventually be surpassed—and to no small degree already has been, in our era of digital cosmopolitanism, alongside a global anti-colonial movement. Entheogens make us more than modern humans, more like cosmic hybrids connected to all life forms; their radical conceptual framework could also destabilize the very idea of "human"—or at least loosen its hold over our cognitive structures.

As European humanism is questioned and dismembered, so will the episteme of Western

science ultimately be decommissioned with
the collapse of its ideological influence over
life forms and their entheogenic integration.
Shamanic cosmology does away with the notion
of Western humanism as the identity structure
for advanced humanity. Through pharmacoeth-
nography, we discover that there are no neutral
positions in pharmacological cosmologies; all
positions and actions belong to an energetic
trajectory and network of life. With every mol-
ecule one consumes, a set of cultural practices is
provoked or quelled—indeed, this is happening
around the world. This insight sheds light on
many other practices such as yoga, meditation,
and psychedelic research, which all have ties to
"shamanic" cosmologies; these are also domains
for Indigenous intellectual property rights that
deserve protection from Western colonization.
We should be careful about taking "peoples'
medicines" without accounting for their cultural
context as an act of appropriation.

There is an entheogenic body-time contained
in mythological cosmologies; this is more than
a metaphor. It should be approached in order
to discern its inherent cognitive potential—
something that extends far beyond the conceptual framework of Western science. Shamans,
ethnopharmacologists, neuro-researchers, and

molecular biologists traverse different cognitive territories that are still part of the same universe. Since 2010 there has been an acceleration in entheogenic vitalism as two cultures come together: European and Indigenous cosmologies join the fractal hyperobjects of nonhuman pharmacological intelligence to produce a more complex theory for entheogenesis. With humankind so fragmented, dispersed, separated into loops and lines of post-digital culture and politics, the time is right for interspecies integration—the move towards a new boundaryless consciousness that enfolds rather than divides.

13

23 lines after Anicka Yi's work
by Taro Hattori

1   I am surrounded by a permeable membrane that separates the inside and the outside.

2   The permeable membrane is structured by perceptions.

3   I am a human.

4   I do not receive the World as it is but very limited aspects of it through a series of perceptions that humans could obtain and preserve.

5   I have these perceptions. 1. Equilibrioceptive (balance) 2. Proprioceptive (movement) 3. Nociceptive (pain and wellness) 4. Tactile (touch) 5. Gustatory (taste) 6. Olfactory (smell) 7. Thermoceptive (warmth, heat, and absence of heat) 8. Visual (documentation of dimensions) 9. Auditory (hearing) 10. Phoneme (language) 11. Thought 12. Ego

6 I receive the world as *Umwelt*. If the moon suddenly disappears, I may simply weep for a few days, but the corals stop breeding.

7 I record the accumulation of information from those perceptions and write a fiction called Self using the faculty of language, numbers, images, indexes, and symbols.

8 "I" need "Thou" to be "I."

9 "We" need "They" to be "We."

10 All of them are in the fiction inside of me and malleable.

11 With certain external stimulations or internal cognitions, "I" becomes "Thou" becomes "We" becomes "They" becomes "I."

12 I am a construct of someone else. I bear strangers within myself.

13 The Mirror Neurons bridge strangers. The We-Mode bridges strangers.

14 Those bridges are surrounded by the "Unknown," and every time I receive an

external stimulation deviant from the cognitive inference, I rewrite the fiction.

15 The Mirror Neurons in the body of "I" respond to and correspond with the body of "Thou."

16 "Thou" said that my body smells like a muskmelon.

17 The body of "We" responds to and corresponds with the body of "They."

18 Body has its own language.

19 The pain has its own language. It reminds me of my body, the body of "Thou," "We," and "They."

20 Body responds to and corresponds with the Flesh of the World, the physicality of the environment.

21 I feel the presence of a deceased friend on a piece of pyrite through the projection of the fiction from Body to the Flesh of the World.

22 Projection of the fiction from Body bridges

between "I" and "Thou," "We," and "They,"
and humans and more-than humans, and
machines.

23 The membrane between them becomes so
permeable and one flows into the other, and
every one of us starts living in the liminal
milieu with unanswered questions.

Inspired by the writings by
     Maurice Merleau-Ponty
     Giacomo Rizzolatti and Laila Craighero
     Rudolf Steiner
     Jakob von Uexküll and Thomas Sebeok
     Victor and Edith Turner
     Martin Buber
     Julia Kristeva
     Karl Friston
     Wafaa Bilal
     Boris C. Bernhardt and Tania Singer
     Susan Sontag
     Mattia Gallotti and Chris D. Frith

Quantum Art Manifesto V
by Yutaka Matsuzawa

The things which can be seen with the eyes now possessed by humankind are all commonplace. At the present juncture, we must change our eyes so that we can begin to see something invisible. First, we must close our eyes, hoping to see something unknown in the depths of our eyes, and try to build that something with will and intelligence. With will and intelligence, we must anticipate seeing that something and become used to it. The something we cannot see now but will become able to see is interesting. In *The Universe Born from Nothing*, Kazuyuki Mogi says, "It has been shown that history is a physical reality of irrational numbers and negative numbers transcending mathematical reality. In particular, discovery of the concept of the reality of negative time and negative energy in the world of mathematics shows great possibilities for anticipating a perceptual world which cannot be seen. This provides a basis for the reality of an empty world."

Preparatory sketches for
new Radiolaria sculptures
by Anicka Yi Studio

what the coral said:

> breathe. breathe. breathe. sing. let that water
> move within you. let it be you. let your every
> cilia dance you into healing. let the warm
> salt water brighten you. your tears. sleep.
> and when you dream of working, sleep again.
> sleep until you dream of floating. dream until
> your edges soft. dream until you birth your-
> self in water singing with the bones of all
> your lost. dream until you breathe not from
> your mouth, not from your nose but through
> your hair and through your skin. dream until
> you claim the ocean. breathe until you feel
> no need to swim. breathe until your dreams
> flow out your brain. breathe and let them in
> your heart. breathe and we will call you again.
> that's a start.

—Alexis Pauline Gumbs, *Dub: Finding Ceremony*
(Duke University Press: 2020), p. 13

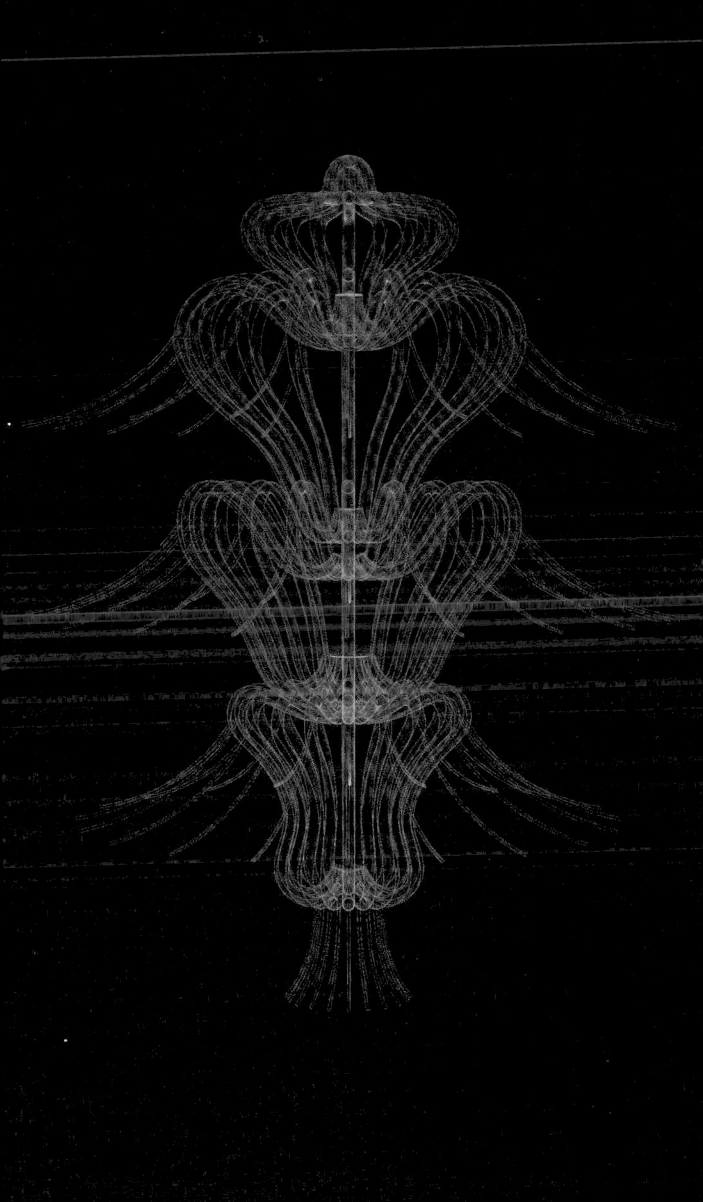

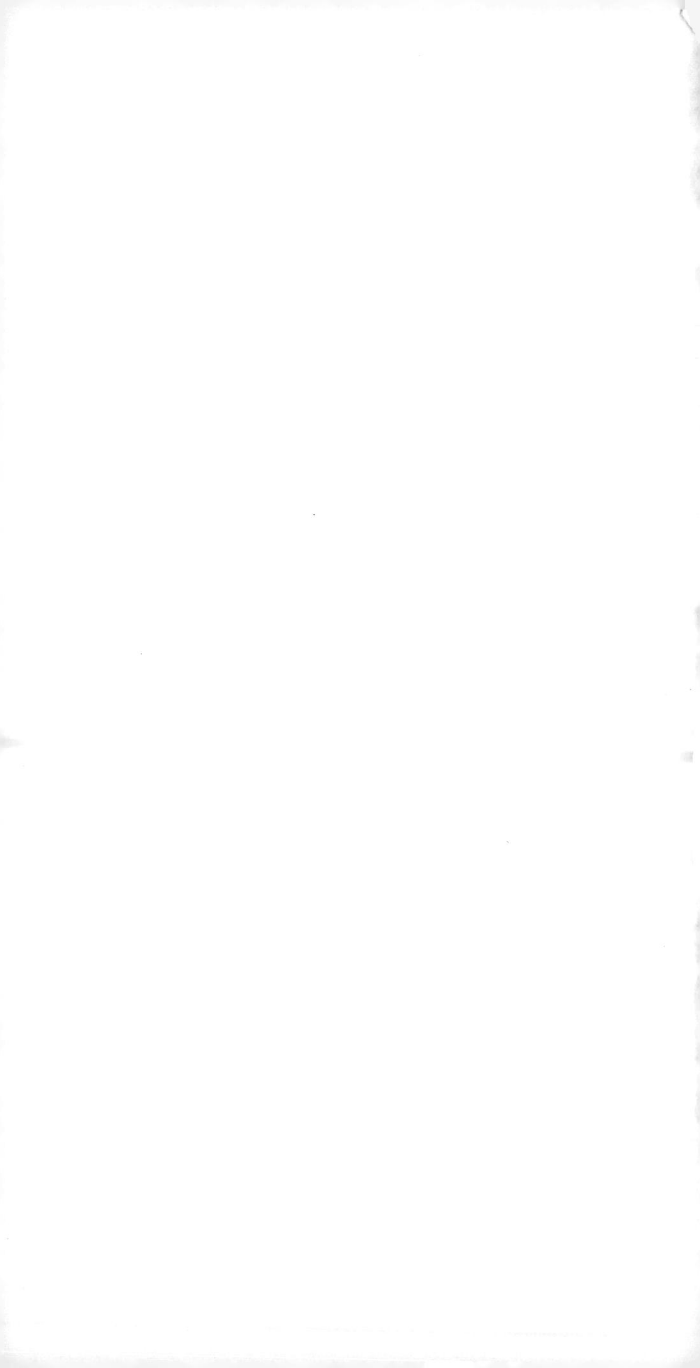

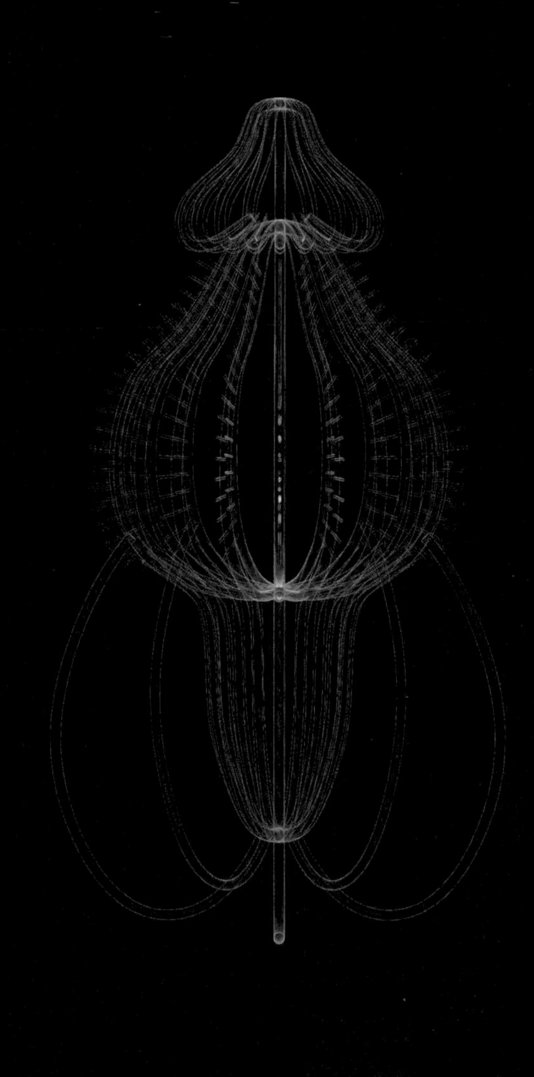

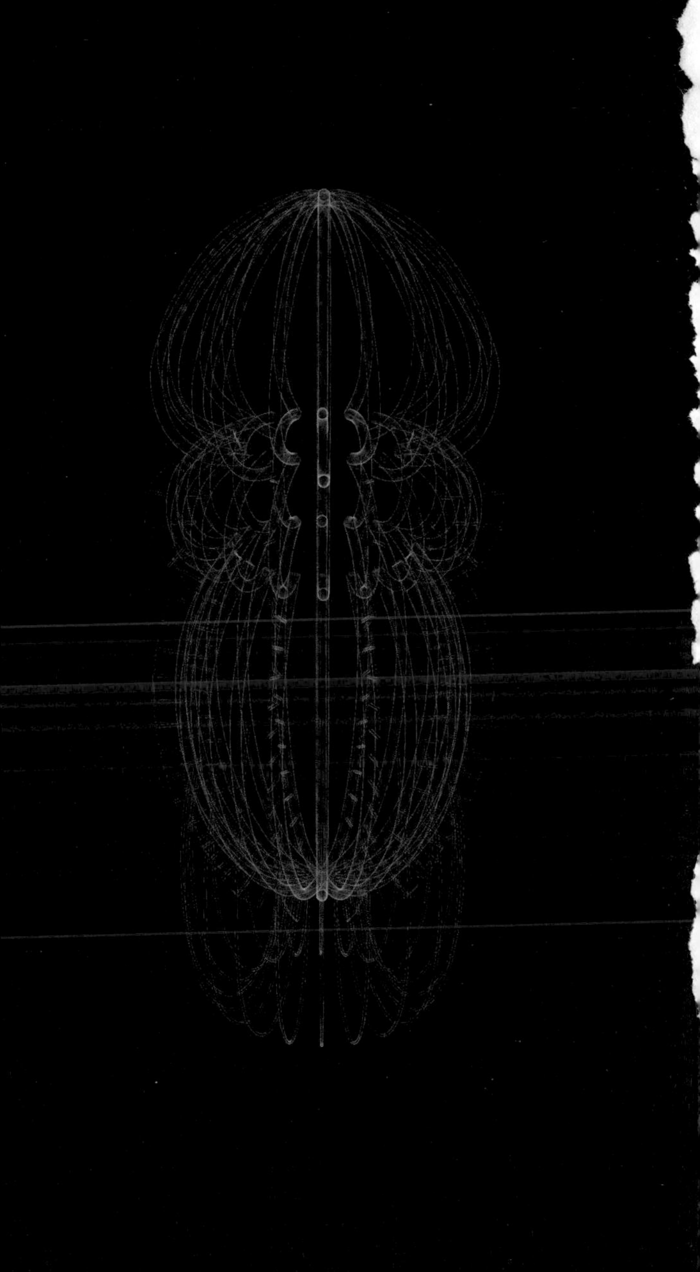

16

Vertical Time / Transversal Time
by Ayesha Hameed

Item

In July 2017, the *New York Times* reported a story about George Church and Seth Shipman, geneticists and researchers at Harvard Medical School, who encoded frames from Eadweard Muybridge's 1878 photographic sequence of a galloping horse into the DNA of a living cell. This encoding was performed using CRISPR, a gene-editing software, which assigned a shade of gray to each of the four molecules composing all configurations of DNA, based on the pixel they represented in Muybridge's image.

The moving image of the galloping horse was found to maintain its integrity over several generations of bacteria. At a molecular level, then, this is an encoding of time in a movie that operates as a witness, a producer of testimony that is made of the same material it bears witness to. The science-fiction fantasy of this encoding goes further: it projects a future where bacterial DNA could record the activity of the cells they

are attached to. One day, bacteria could act as
a black box recording the illnesses and cellular
life of the bodies they live in. Time, witnessing,
and bacteria become intertwined and, as a result,
detached from their referents at a molecular level.
Together, they tell another set of stories.

Item

Dust report. The oldest records of dust transport
date from 1965 in Ragged Point, Barbados. Trade
winds blowing across the Atlantic, from the Sahel
to the Caribbean and beyond, make up about 70
percent of the global distribution of dust. It takes
a week for dust to cross the ocean and disinte-
grate in the friction of its flight. These grains
of dust are rich in iron and phosphorus. Dust
travels across the Atlantic, spreading iron into the
ocean's carbon cycle and providing marine micro-
organisms with a vital micronutrient.[1] This dust
also forms deposits in the soil in the Bahamas
and Caribbean—adding phosphorus and other
nutrients to the soil all the way into the Amazon
basin, and much-needed iron deposits in the
Atlantic Ocean.[2] Before merging with land or sea,
airborne dust has an impact on the weather and
climate of the Caribbean. It can affect the growth
of cyclones and the temperature of sea surfaces,

which in turn could affect hurricane activity
and cloud microphysics.[3] Dust is also linked to
health issues. Throughout the Caribbean, there
is widespread asthma, which might be connected
to the prevalence of dust. Half of the dust that
crosses from the Sahel is less than 2.5 µm in
diameter, which is categorized by United States
Environmental Protection Agency standards
as "respirable" or inhalable. In epidemiological
studies, respirable dust has been correlated with
asthma, chronic bronchitis, and other severe
respiratory symptoms.[4]

Dust moves both horizontally across the
ocean and land, and vertically into the depths of
the earth, the sea, and into human bodies and
lungs. Regarding the latter, one cannot help but
recall the words of Bataille: "The storytellers
have not realized that the Sleeping Beauty would
have awoken covered in a thick layer of dust;
nor have they envisaged the sinister spiders'
webs that would have been torn apart at the first
movement of her red tresses. Meanwhile dismal
sheets of dust constantly invade earthly habi-
tations and uniformly defile them: as if it were
a matter of making ready attics and old rooms
for the imminent occupation of the obsessions,
phantoms, specters that the decayed odor of old
dust nourishes and intoxicates."[5]

*

Question. What is the time of dust and of cellular matter?

Answer.
Here are intimations that the machine of the Plantationocene not only moves horizontally across land and sea but also plummets into the depths of body tissue and molecular life. What role does the CRISPR cells' movie play in the machine of the Plantationocene? This can be at first understood by returning to Benítez-Rojo: "In truth, the field in which Chaos may be observed is extremely vast, for it includes all phenomena that depend on the passage of time; Chaos looks toward everything that repeats, reproduces, grows, decays, unfolds, flows, spins, vibrates, seethes; it is as interested in the evolution of the solar system as in the stock market's crashes, as involved in cardiac arrhythmia as in the novel or in myth."[6] [Antonio] Benítez-Rojo's description of Chaos as operating on the register of both the body and the solar system, that is, as both scalar and embodied, comes close to the multiplication of time that the machine of the Plantationocene—with its own enslaved bodies—needs to take into account. In the

132

first instance, this scalar time has the quality of verticality; it probes both the depths of tissue matter and territory.

To move deeper into tissue is to move in time. This is a relationship with the sediment. Dust writ large is a temporal symptom of the passage of time and of accumulating sedimentary layers. Dust in its microcosmic form is what we breathe in or what makes breath difficult.

Kathryn Yusoff's notion of "geologic time" implicates this temporal conjunction of body and territory that highlights its verticality. Geologic time recognizes that our origins are interconnected with geologic sedimentations, and that as a species we humans will end up as a set of sedimented fossils as well. The shock of this confrontation of origins and ends produces the spectral beginnings of time travel. In imagining ourselves as fossils, humans become "an object that has collided with its specter to provide its own haunting."[7]

In other words, this horizon of ends produces a kind of collision of self with the specter of a future self, but this also plays out in the temporal awareness of the sedimentation of geologic strata. There is, consequently, a futurity built into the geologic strata, Yusoff argues, and this plays out on the terrain of the archaeological,

the verticality of the cross-section of the earth,
moving vertically downward:

> To imagine ourselves a fossil is to become
> the body/thing that is abandoned to time
> and given over to the chaotic churnings
> of the earth. Implicit in this imagining is a
> model of the earth as strata: vertical rather
> than horizontal territory; intensified by the
> passage of time; in layers that press hard
> on the possibilities of forms that become
> fragmented in time and material integrity.
> The fossil then is an abandoned being that
> suddenly in the midst of the present recon-
> figures the possibilities of times, of past and
> future, and like a line of flight thrown from
> some prehistoric world it offers a hitherto
> unimaginable direction to thought and
> becoming. This is the temporal and spatial
> scene in which fossils speak.[8]

It is this verticality that reconfigures the fossil,
bringing into its composition both past and
future. The complicity between body and
sediment, or body and the geologic/geographic,
goes even further through the medium of bone.
It cuts transversally into the body akin to
the movie made up of bacterial sequences.

"De Landa reminds us that the origins of our bodily composition are a form of mineralization that is always on the threshold between the biological vitality of bone and the dead matter of the fossil, and ready to cross back into the geologic record at a moment's notice."[9]

Scaled down. In their spatial study of police violence and urban planning in the United States, Lindsey Dillon and Julie Sze connect dust and the ability to breathe as an "important spatiality through which to critique contemporary relations of power."[10] Dillon and Sze reexamine Eric Garner's murder in a choke hold by the police. Garner, an asthma sufferer, repeated "I can't breathe" before dying. His last words became a key slogan in the Black Lives Matter movement, but they also resonate with environmental justice on a broader level: Dillon and Sze describe the prevalence of asthma sufferers in Black communities, and connect this to urban renewal, including highway construction, which increases exposure to air pollution. Consequently, there is a high correlation between race and incidences of asthma.

Asthma, like dust, is created by factors that are both external and internal to bodies, they argue, as are illnesses like hypertension, diabetes, and obesity. The authors argue that this is inextricable from racial segregation in the United States.

Garner's death is an environmental and racial issue with a long history. Being able to breathe is a matter of racial privilege: "In this vein, we interpret the phrase 'I can't breathe' as condensing the histories of persistent patterns of pollution and police violence, both of which have denied breath and healthy breathing spaces to low-income communities of color. In this sense, the inability to breathe can be understood as both a metaphor and material reality of racism, which constrains not just life choices and opportunities, but the environmental conditions of life itself."[11] To deny breath is to deny the humanity of one trying to breathe. Scaled down, the particulate matter of dust infiltrates the body, and makes indissoluble the transition from dust to membrane. Scaled up, the dust of the highway and of urban renewal provides the topography for dusty lungs. Bones become fossils and back again, dust enters lungs, carpets, cities, becomes a weapon no less systemic than the choke hold laying Eric Garner to the ground.

Breathing in dust particles juxtaposes two temporalities: the future/anterior vectors of the fossil that is ingested, and the gasping body that is mired in the present and in crisis. This is an incursion of one time—of fossils (slow, future/anterior)—into another time, that of

the body-at-this moment (rapid, present).
Materially, dust crosses the membrane dividing
the body from its environment and becomes
part of the body. Temporally, future and anterior
time infiltrate the membrane of the present in
crisis.

There is no air, only dust. When there is no
breath, it is death.

*

Question. How to plot this in island time?

Answer.
Drexciyan bodies skew this equation by changing the substance of breath from air into water.
They can breathe, but breathing is something
else in an improbable time.

Water is made of strata that are sedimented
and carry portents of other times, both anticipa-
tory and remembered. This is material. Nicholas
Mirzoeff, in his 2017 essay "Below the Water:
Black Lives Matter and Revolutionary Time,"
follows the trajectory of cyclones across the
Atlantic, and points out that the direction of
the winds follows that of the slave ships several
centuries ago.

After Hurricane Katrina devastated New Orleans in 2005, there was much discussion about the fact that hurricanes seem to follow the same route taken by the slave ships. It was said that spirits from the Middle Passage (like the Haitian *lwa* Simbi) had destroyed the city in their anger over slavery. Why would the spirits destroy African-American homes over slavery, rather than those of slavers? They are nonhuman and think differently. They want to take their human counterparts "back to Africa." In Kreyol, that connection is called *anba dlo* (beneath the water).

This nauticalization of Black Lives Matter forms the creation of what he calls "revolutionary time below the water." Mirzoeff explains:

Revolutionary time allows for the unexpunged potential of a moment to be reanimated. A dialectical image catches such potential and contains it, waiting for the moment in which it can again be seen for what it is. Revolutionary time has never left the place of possibility, rather than trying to contain it in norms and hierarchies. In revolutionary time, actors experience the future in real time because the intensity of their contact with others takes place so quickly that it is to experience in days what otherwise might take months or years. Revolutionary time is more like cosmological time than it is like capitalist time.[12]

For Mirzoeff, it is no strange coincidence that the routes of the slave ships are retraced by the indiscriminate destructive force of hurricanes and cyclones, as a kind of return of matter in waiting. It undoes the dictates of clock time in industrial modes of production under capitalism. Instead, it is the recapitulation of a time in the past that has reversed its force and direction of destruction, drawing from the violent movement of the slave ships it retraces and reappropriates. This primordial dialectical image captures in its force the bodies of descendants of the enslaved, taking them into the ocean, across the ocean, and below the ocean. This is the labor of *anba dlo*. Here, a gesture of translation is enacted in moving across the ocean, it is a spatiotemporal leap that reckons with the past while cycling the future into the present.

Fossils that connect bodies to their environments find their counterpart in the materialization of underwater space. Like geologic time, sedimentations in the sea can be read temporally and vertically. The mineralization of bodies in water is part of what Christina Sharpe calls "residence time": the persistence, at a molecular level, of enslaved bodies decomposing in water, solids turning to salinity as bones turn to calcium, and vice versa. This is the temporalization of organic matter becoming inorganic and flipping back again.

The threshold between ocean and body is not only eroded in the mineralization of bodies but also by rethinking the threshold of what constitutes living matter in the life of the ocean. [Elizabeth] DeLoughrey describes how the sea meets the liveliness of the human body in its mutability. This materializes the strata of water just as the erosion of bodies in residence time temporalizes them:

> The discourse of the Anthropocene positions humans as a geological force, yet the ocean seems to be our proxy. This raises questions as to the mutability between humans and the seas. While we recognize an anthropogenic climate, new science is suggesting a rather anthropomorphic ocean—perhaps even a super organism. Water's mutability, measured in picoseconds, means that it changes its molecular structure around one trillion times

a second and has been likened to a network. Recent work on the ocean as superorganism has focused on the blurring between chemistry and living beings, as well as the "bacterial networking" [...] of the ocean's microbial communities.[13]

This blurring of what constitutes the threshold of life has a temporal register, the picosecond axis of molecular change in the sea. Returning to the molecular and to the measuring of units of time in order to map the constitution of a maritime space also returns us to a Drexciyan pivot: the possibility of human fetuses adapting from amniotic fluid to seawater, and therefore able to breathe underwater after being born.

As Outi and I were looking at the water tanks in Seili, she told me she was thinking about my remark about Drexciyans adapting to living underwater, and that I was wrong. Like the seaweed we were looking at, he thought that Drexciyans would have acclimatized to living in the sea. There was no change at the level of their DNA; rather, it was a stretching of the existing characteristics of these unborn children. At first I was puzzled, as developing gills and breathing underwater, and subsequently developing flippers, did seem like a more fundamental change. Later on, I remembered recapitulation theory: that ontogeny recapitulates phylogeny; that as it develops, the fetus represents each stage of evolution. What if the fetus just got off at an earlier stop on the evolutionary bus that it replicates in miniature in the womb? Recapitulation of an earlier stage of development to an improbable acclimatization to living underwater: moving simultaneously forward and backward in time. In other words, the mutability of the matter of bodies and of the matter of water are immanently time-traveling states. DeLoughrey again, with reference to Hawaiian and Maori understandings of temporality:

> Time is registered by a syntactic movement between present- and past- continuous tense by a narrator who, in the first line of the story, is "thinking back" to the omens before the launch, and then is interrupted by the present voice, an "I" who is "balanced on the end bollard" [...]. This dynamic earthly change is [...] being experienced in the interwoven tenses of an immediate present and past. This highlights the experience of climate change as a contemporaneous experience in the Pacific, as well as Maori epistemologies that position the past in front while the future is behind.[14]

This is vertical time, but plotted transversally. Narration is disrupted, time is mutable with the mutability of the water and the intermediate past and present blurring into one another.

Notes

1   See Joseph M. Prospero and Olga L. Mayol-Bracero, "Understanding the Transport and Impact of African Dust on the Caribbean Basin," *Bulletin of the American Meteorological Society* 94, no. 9 (2013): 1329–37; and Joseph M. Prospero, "Saharan Dust Impacts and Climate Change," *Oceanography* 19, no. 2 (2006): 60–61.

2   Prospero, "Saharan Dust Impacts," 61.

3   Prospero and Mayol-Bracero, "African Dust on the Caribbean Basin," 1331.

4   Prospero, "Saharan Dust Impacts," 60.

5   Georges Bataille, "Dust," in *Encyclopaedia Acephalica*, ed. Alastair Brotchie, trans. Iain White (Arias Press, 1995), 423.

6   Antonio Benítez-Rojo, *The Repeating Island: The Caribbean and the Postmodern Perspective*, trans. James E. Maraniss, 2nd ed. (Duke University Press, 1997), 3.

7   Kathryn Yusoff, "Geologic Life: Prehistory,

Climate, Futures, or Do Fossils Dream of Geologic Life" (unpublished manuscript, April 2012), II, https://eprints.lancs.ac.uk /id/eprint/73620/1/GeologicLife_April2012 _yusoff.pdf.

8   Yusoff, 7.

9   Yusoff, 5.

10 Lindsey Dillon and Julie Sze, "Police Power and Particulate Matters: Environmental Justice and the Spatialities of In/securities in U.S. Cities," *English Language Notes* 54, no. 2 (Fall/Winter 2016): 14.

11 Dillon and Sze, 19.

12 Nicholas Mirzoeff, "Below the Water: Black Lives Matter and Revolutionary Time," *e-flux journal*, no. 79 (February 2017), https://www.e-flux.com/journal/79/94164 /below-the-water-black-lives-matter-and -revolutionary-time/.

13 Elizabeth DeLoughrey, "Ordinary Futures: Interspecies Worldings in the Anthropocene," in *Global Ecologies and the Environmental Humanities: Postcolonial Approaches*, ed. Elizabeth DeLoughrey, Jill Didur, and Anthony Carrigan (Routledge, 2015), 358.

14 DeLoughrey, 259.

17

Memoirs of a Spacewoman
by Naomi Mitchison

It was quite a problem to get through to those radial entities. Naturally I spent some time in the most unobtrusive observing while I thought out the best communication techniques to use. Their main organs were, of course, central and not orientated in any direction. I soon became sure that any unevenness in the peripheral ring of brain-plus-eye material was looked upon as a blemish, but one was left in uncertainty as to whether this was supposed to be moral or physical.

They also wore at times a kind of flimsy artificial covering which could either protect the ring or make it more obvious, and which appeared to be kept below the body, or possibly to be exuded from the under part. It clung to one's fingers if one touched it, and had a smell which was entirely new to me and difficult to assess. It was extremely hard to know what kind of thing this was without interference. And I was being very, very careful about that, all the more as it was my first world.

After a time, however, I realized that I must concentrate on what went on during periods of a rather strange activity in which first of all one radiate would move under a shelter and start to turn, first in one direction, then in another; apparently the direction in which they began occurred entirely at random, or at any rate we never found any evidence to the contrary. I am almost certain that this was a kind of reversion towards spirality. In our world, species which spiral do so in one direction only, but I do not think this would have been the case with the ancestors of my radiates. I found a small shell-producing form of life in this world, and was interested to see that its spiral went either way. At any rate, the dance would begin with one individual. Then another would become aware of this and approach. The two would lock together like cog-wheels, an "arm" into a hollow. Then, usually quite rapidly, others would appear so that in a matter of half an hour there would be a dense carpet of them, the inner ones locked together, the outer ones apparently in some agitation attempting to get inward, especially if there were so many that the shelter could not cover them. Had these creatures been descended from six-armed ancestors, the putting together would have been easier; as it was there were always gaps in the perfection of the carpet, even if the "arms" were retracted, expanded, or otherwise adjusted. And it seemed as though the object was for all to come close and quiet and untroubled.

When this was achieved for a moment, the membranes covering the eyes, which were deep bluish-green in contrast to the general brownish-yellow of the body color, shut down and the brain ring with its marked nodules at the central arm nerves appeared to flatten. We had some knowledge of the anatomy of these creatures owing to the fact that we occasionally saw one that had been killed by a type of insectoid enemy, not unlike mosquitoes, but up to thirty centimeters long, with extremely hard sucking jaws, which dropped on to the radiates from above. These were what we called jags. They appeared to be so nearly without consciousness of any kind that we were prepared to count them provisionally as not-life. Of course, one can communicate with all forms of life, however destructive and without consciousness; but that time has not come. Meanwhile it had enabled us on this world to do a dissection and preservation of one of the inhabitants. We could only hope that we had not interfered with any death or burial rites.

It was against these jags, we thought, that our radiates built their decorated shelters. Meanwhile, the jags dropped jaws first on to the eye ring, killing in a matter of minutes. None of them had actually attacked one of us, but there was always the possibility. Several times they had plummeted onto pieces of apparatus that had some glistening parts, which might have appeared to them as eyes. We were taking no risks.

Once I had settled down with the radiates, I tried out various means of communication until at last I got my contact. It took me a long time, I remember. Nowadays I would probably have managed it all much quicker and with more certain jumps towards the solution of my problem, but after all, this was my first world. There were days when I felt completely baffled, but I just could not go back and say to T'o M'Kasi, or indeed to any of the others, that I had been unable to get through.

I did meanwhile make a number of observations that supplemented those other members of the expedition were making. I had decided that I had better, as far as possible, go around on hands and knees so as to be at the same aesthetic level as the rest of the inhabitants. Had I not done so, I would probably not have realized

the nature of some of the movable artifacts.
In fact, I could not always make out what, if
anything, they were used for, but could admire
them. I was looking at a rounded object in some
material that I did not recognize, but which
had decorations inside it, of much the same
kind that, from time to time in human aesthetic
history, workers in glass have been proud to
produce. It was apparently something that was
rolled round the eye ring by a muscular ripple.
I could not see that it was in any way what one
might call useful. And suddenly my aesthetic
admiration appeared to meet an echo. I realized
I had got through.

As usual in communication problems, the
first step was the most difficult. Once one saw
what kind of rapport should be looked for, it
was a matter of rapid assemblement of data. I
had, after all, had the training. At one stage in
my solution—or rather our joint solution, for
the radiates were as eager from their side as
I was from mine—I had a piece of luck. I saw
one of the jags hurtling down and managed
to kill it in flight. Oddly enough, I had never
killed anything before. Terra, after all, is clear of
enemies. I knew the jags counted as not-life, but
all the same I was shocked at my own action.
Not so the radiates.

Well, I won't bore you with my observations. The final findings of the expedition are all naturally in the Journal. I remember I made a most ludicrous mistake about their sex life! This was corrected in a later edition; it was all due to my own anthropomorphizing. I had been warned about it often enough, but one never knows quite how these things will take one. Doubtless my subconscious drive was firmly fastened on myself and T'o.

However, my conscious concentration was all on the radiates. Gradually over a period of weeks I developed communication, first from generalized approval or disapproval and the simple harmonics to more complex and precise and mental aesthetic or mathematical statements. Then gradually we got on, once they themselves were cooperating completely, to further developments.

I had, of course, like a dancer, to adapt myself to my communicators. That's the kind of reason why, as I've said, I believe communication science is so essentially womanly. It fits one's basic sex patterns. And the more I adapted to them, the more out of tune I became with my own normal concepts. Turning over on my mattress—I had one of those rather special ones then that fold into nothing and foam at a

touch of any atmosphere; nowadays I meditate
and don't need one—even that simple choice
involving right or left seemed unnatural. Right
hand or left—impossible alternations!

In communication, as, of course, you realize,
by the constant succession of a or b, a or b
choices, snap judgments and actions can be
made as rapidly as possible in the semi-
intuitive technique we have all learned, which
is both mental and manual since it also involves
instruments. I found these choice successions
increasingly difficult to make. It was like walking
in loose sand, a drag of other concepts.

One is so used to a two-sided brain, two eyes,
two ears, and so on that one takes the whole
thing and all that stems from it for granted.
Incorrectly, but inevitably. My radiates had an
entirely different outlook. As I got to know them
better, I realized that in many ways they were
highly—in our phrase—"civilized." But they
never thought in terms of either-or. It began
to seem to me very peculiar that I should do so
myself, and that so many of my judgments were
paired: good and evil, black or white, to be or
not to be. Even while one admitted that moral
and intellectual judgments were shifting and
temporary, they had still seemed to exist. Above
all, judgments of scientific precision. But after a

certain amount of communication with the radiates all this smudged out. If alternative means,
not one of two, but one, two, three or four out
of five, then action is complicated and slowed
to the kind of tempo and complexity that is
appropriate to an organism with many hundreds
of what were in evolutionary time fairly simple
suckers and graspers, but which in development
have adapted themselves for locomotion, food
retention, tool-handling, the finer delicacies of
touch, and probably for other purposes of which
I only became partly aware. It thus came about
that with no sense of awkwardness, two or more
choices could be made more or less conflicting
though never opposite. Gradually I found myself
getting into the same state of mind.

As I got to know my radiates as individuals—
always a little difficult with a completely other
species and one tends to memorize individuality
by inessential markings and deformations and
such—the thing got more difficult. They did not
name themselves as we Terrans do, and as we
are apt to imagine most other worlds do. There
were, however, group names shading into one
another. Slowly I began to forget my own name.

18

Before It Fades
Text by Karen Cheung
Images by Heesoo Kwon

In *De memoria et reminiscentia* (circa 350 BC), Aristotle describes memory as a state or affection of either perception or conception, conditioned by the lapse of time. The organ with the faculty of perceiving time is capable of possessing memory. We can now analyze Aristotle's theory at a neuron level—the collection of neurons and the synapses between them within an intertwining network. Our fragmentary childhood memories from before age three are analogous to home videos recorded before our directorial debut. These low-fi tapes are uncatalogued and unedited. Most of them are lost in the attic or basement, but those rediscovered at an older age are read as fictional films. Scientists have suggested attributions of this phenomenon known as "childhood amnesia" correlate with stages of brain development. The high rate of neuron production in the hippocampus—the brain region primarily involved with memory—during our young years may disrupt existing networks of already formed memories.[1] But unlike footage taped over and unrecoverable, latent traces of early memories can survive, in particular those with strong emotional associations. Through the process of remembering repeatedly, new details of events can emerge and alter. Dr. Michael S. Gazzaniga's studies of brain lateralization in the 1980s and 90s discovered how the left hemisphere encodes information through coherent narratives, sometimes by inserting assumptions and judgments to see the full picture.[2] As persuasive storytellers, many of our first memories incorporate fictional autobiographical elements.[3] Gazzaniga labeled this system of our brain as the interpreter. When listening to stories with greater elaboration of emotions and references to time, these past events are remembered and recalled better.[4]

Artist Heesoo Kwon first discovered home video tapes in boxes of nearly abandoned objects recovered by her mother. Watching recordings of her family and herself at a young age from a third person point of view was a peculiar experience for the artist, particularly during a time of introspection with attempts to process her ordeals with Catholicism and patriarchy. Kwon's experience of excavating her family archives had a profound impact on her work. Not only did it lead to the genesis of *Leymusoom*, an auto-biographical feminist religion she initiated in 2017 as a form of personal resistance against misogyny, she also started positioning herself as an anthropologist and archivist who utilizes technologies to investigate and reinterpret her family histories.[5] Since her birth and until age six, Kwon and her extended family lived in one house located in Ilwon-dong, Seoul, South Korea. Her father frequently traveled for his career during this time so this household mostly comprised four generations of women. Despite his periodic absence, most photo portraits of women and the seemingly tender and joyful scenes of everyday life pictured in this family home were captured by the artist's father. She later learned her father's gaze in the family photographs greatly differed from her mother's experience. An image of Kim washing dishes over the kitchen sink may seem commonplace amongst family photos, but what was not cap-tured on camera, nor obvious to Kwon, was her mother's weariness from the incessant domestic labor performed.[6]

For her experimental documentary *Video Blues* (2019), the filmmaker Emma Tusell ana-lyzed in granular detail home video footage recorded by her father in the 1980s to search

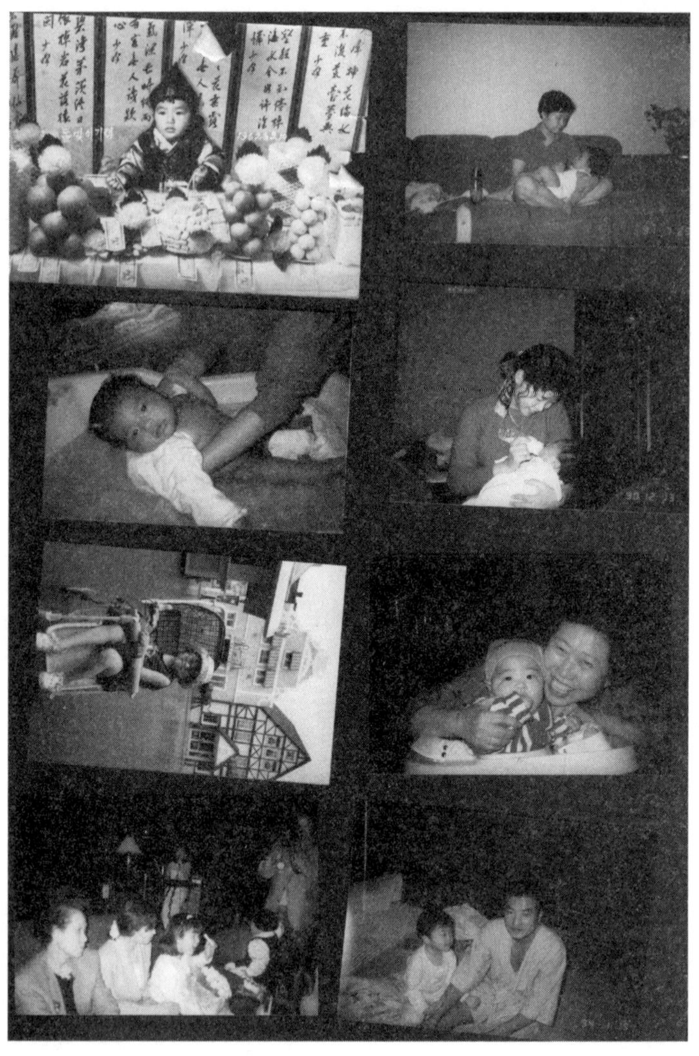

for answers about her parents' separation, complex family dynamics, and her own identity. She used various video editing and manipulation techniques—freeze-frame, rewinding, changing playback speed, compiling different sequences—alongside a narrative dialogue with her partner to create new meaning in these old images. But Tusell did not attempt to zoom into the footage because how these images were framed provided insight into her father's experience. Tusell's father used his camera's telephoto lens for certain images, but when he zooms out, the actual distance between the videographer and the subject is revealed. It reaffirms this sense of closeness was all but an illusion. The photographic series *Premolt* and video *A Ritual for Metamorphosis* (both 2019) were Heesoo Kwon's first attempts at reframing her family history in her work. She inserted digital avatars of herself and Leymusoom into family photographs and home videos captured by her father. They became witnesses who disrupted the patriarchal and religious rituals practiced in her childhood home. Kwon sought a different approach in reinterpreting her family archive in her photographic series *Leymusoom Firefly, Il-won-dong* 1990–1996 (2023). Instead of creating interruptions, she was essentially interested

in what Tusell was exploring in her work—the
realities depicted in images and their continuity with other possibilities that exist off-screen.
She abandoned the distinct visual language of
her digital avatars and opted to work with AI
to manipulate her images. Kwon used a new
feature in the image-editing software Adobe
Photoshop that can either expand the borders of
an image by generating additional out-of-frame
content that matches the lighting, style, and
perspective of the original photo, or completely
replace parts of an image based on simple text
prompts from the user. This tool is powered by
Adobe Firefly, a generative AI model trained
using other photographs from the stock image
asset database Adobe Stock. Because Firefly is
informed by and makes aesthetic decisions based
on a repository of public images, Kwon considers Firefly a collaborator with some agency
rather than just a mindless editing tool. Each
photograph drawn from Kwon's family archive
is the foundational layer of the image. The artist
selects a small section of the photo and prompts
Adobe Firefly to generate an extended border
without giving any descriptive text. The AI
model then provides Kwon with three content
options to create a generative layer. Her selec-
tion is based on her best recollection of interior

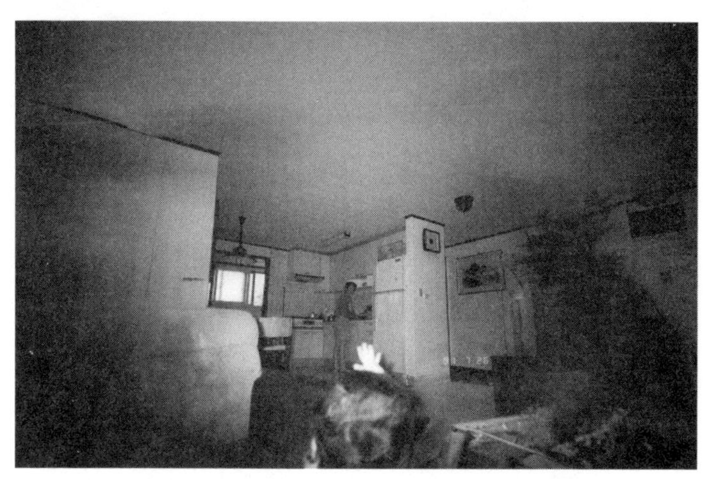

spaces and the objects and people in them. She
repeats this process until enough layers are
generated to make the scene appear complete. It
began as a slow image-making process, as sometimes Kwon needed to reselect certain sections
so AI would generate more relevant content.
She soon realized her difficulty in recalling each
room of her childhood home, but was able to
spatially map their locations in relation to one
another. She started to fixate on certain interior
details from her memory to help with her selec-
tions, such as the carving patterns on a wooden
side table.

Our domestic spaces are sites of protection
that have a unique psychological effect on us. In
The Poetics of Space (1957), philosopher Gaston
Bachelard observes that memories of home have
a different tonality than the ones of the outside
world. We don't attempt to recall these memories as historians, but more akin to poets, who
express them through emotions and dreams.
The laborious act of retracing the interiors of
her childhood home was strangely therapeutic
for Kwon, even resembling a form of hypnosis
that allowed her to reimagine her earliest memories. After processing a few images, the collaboration with Firefly became more intuitive and
natural, but the results are uncanny reconstruc-

tions of the artist's family home. The discernable
vignettes, high contrast lighting, and cool tones
create haunting images that are mysteriously
captivating. But then you begin to notice the
elongated furniture and repeated appliances,
the disproportion between the scale of spaces
and household objects, and perhaps are able to
distinguish the artificial figures and objects from
the ones in Kwon's past.

 L_F-B-2023_I-D_C1-B1_1994 (2023) captures the rare sight of Kwon at a young age with
her father. The artist's mother was not pictured
in this family portrait, as Kwon speculated she
was the photographer behind the camera. AI
also took notice of her absence and concluded
that another person was missing from the image.
It rendered a physical artifact on the left side
of the original family photo into a fragmented
figure with feminine characteristics and
similar facial features as Kwon and her father.
A hypothesis can be made that AI considers a
complete family unit to consist of three members—a mother, father, and child—and it
learned this through recognizing patterns from
public stock images. Curator Okwui Enwezor
argued in his seminal text *Archive Fever:
Photography Between History and the Monument*
(2008) that when everyday users can distribute

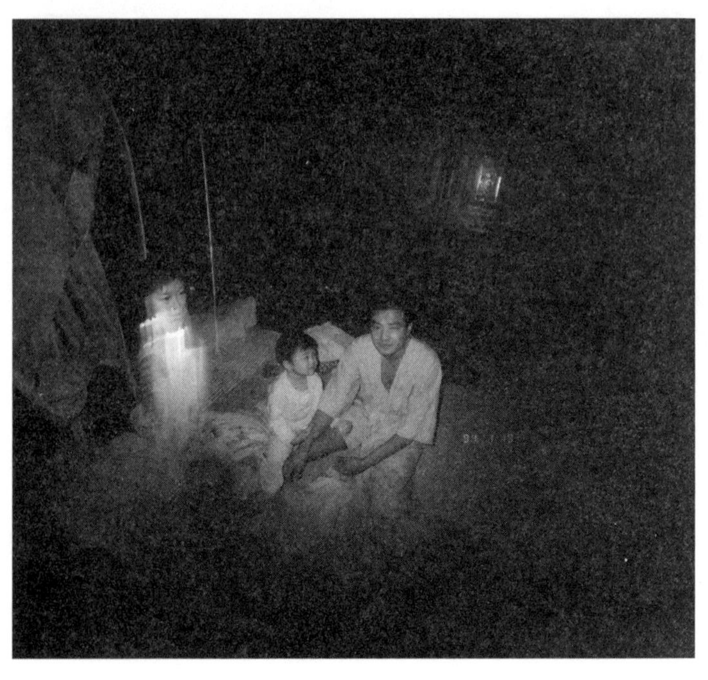

archival content across unregulated fields of image sharing, "the photograph becomes the sovereign analogue of identity, memory, and history, joining past and present, virtual and real, thus giving the photographic document the aura of an anthropological artifact and the authority of a social instrument." As the artist's collaborator and hypnotist, AI brought an artificial woman figure back into the picture to stand in for her mother.

Kwon's photographs form a phantasmagoria of her childhood memories that allow her to perceive her childhood in a different light through reconstructions of her family home. The gradual process of extending family photos allows Kwon to process her childhood memories at the same tempo we adopt to remember and remember again. Each generative layer created reveals a new memory fragment, whether fictional or truthful, and becomes less important as new narratives of the artist's past emerge. Even without her digital avatars, Kwon can liberate her ancestors and herself from familial and historical trauma rooted in patriarchy through these reimagined childhood scenes.

Notes

1   Suk-Yu Yau, Ang Li and Kwok-Fai So,
    "Involvement of adult hippocampal neuro-
    genesis in learning and forgetting," *Neural
    Plasticity* (2015), article 717958.
2   Benedict Carey, "Decoding the Brain's
    Cacophony," *New York Times*, October 3,
    2011.
3   Shazia Akhtar et al., "Fictional First
    Memories," *Psychological Science* vol. 29, 10
    (2018): 1612–1619.
4   Elaine Reese et al., "Looking back to the
    future: Māori and Pakeha mother-child birth
    stories," *Child development* vol. 79, no. 1
    (2008): 114–25.
5   Conversation with the artist, August 11, 2023.
6   Conversation with the artist, August 19, 2023.

19

The Indebted
by Cathy Park Hong

I bring up Korea to collapse the proximity between *here* and *there*. Or as activists used to say, "I am here because you were there."

I am here because you vivisected my ancestral country in two. In 1945, two fumbling mid-ranking American officers who knew nothing about the country used a *National Geographic* map as reference to arbitrarily cut a border to make North and South Korea, a division that eventually separated millions of families, including my own grandmother from her family. Later, under the flag of liberation, the United States dropped more bombs and napalm in our tiny country than during the entire Pacific campaign against Japan during World War II. A fascinating little-known fact about the Korean War is that an American surgeon, David Ralph Millard, stationed there to treat burn victims, invented a double-eyelid surgical procedure to make Asian eyes look Western, which he ended up testing on Korean sex workers so they could be more attractive to

GIs. Now, it's the most popular surgical procedure for women in South Korea. My ancestral country is just one small example of the millions of lives and resources you have sucked from the Philippines, Cambodia, Honduras, Mexico, Iraq, Afghanistan, Nigeria, El Salvador, and many, many other nations through your forever wars and transnational capitalism that have mostly enriched shareholders in the States. Don't talk to me about gratitude.

I was never satisfied with those immigrant talking points about "not belonging" and "the sense of in-betweenness." It seemed rigid and rudimentary, like I just need the right GPS coordinates to find myself. But I also understand the impulse to search for some origin myth of the self, even if it's shaped by the stories told to us, which is why I keep returning to Seoul in my memories, to historical facts that are obscure to most and obvious to few, to try to find better vantage points to justify my feelings here. In Seoul, I still found myself cleaved, but at least it wasn't reduced to broad American talking points. At least the "arsenal of complexes" that Frantz Fanon talks about was laid bare.

Upon my return to the United States, the air thinned; my breath shallowed. As the scholar Seo-Young Chu puts it, I was exiled back to the uncanny valley, where I was returned to my silicon mold and looked out of monolid eyes. To be a writer, then, is to fill myself in with content. To make myself, and by proxy other Asian Americans, more human and a little more relevant to American culture. But that's not enough for me.

Poetry is a forgiving medium for anyone who's had a strained relationship with English. Like the stutterer who pronounces their words flawlessly through song, the immigrant writes their English beautifully through poetry. The poet Louise Glück called the lyric a ruin. The lyric as ruin is an optimal form to explore the racial condition, because our unspeakable losses can be captured through the silences built into the lyric fragment. I have relied on those silences, maybe too much, leaving a blank space for the sorrows that would otherwise be reduced by words. "It is horrible to be tangible inside capital," said the poet Jos Charles. I used to think I'd rather leave a blank space for my pain than have it be easily summed up for consumption. But by turning to prose, I am cluttering that silence to try to anatomize my feelings about a racial identity that I still can't examine as a writer without fretting that I have caved to my containment.

Our respective racial containment isolates us from each other, enforcing our thoughts that our struggles are too specialized, unrelatable to anyone else except others in our group, which is why making myself, and by proxy other Asian Americans, more human is not enough for me. I want to destroy the universal. I want to rip it down. It is not whiteness but our contained condition that is universal, because *we* are the global majority. By *we* I mean nonwhites, the formerly colonized; survivors, such as Native Americans whose ancestors have already lived through end times; migrants and refugees living through end times currently, fleeing the droughts and floods and gang violence reaped by climate change that's been brought on by Western empire.

In Hollywood, whites have churned out dystopian fantasies by imagining *themselves* as slaves and refugees in the future. In *Blade Runner 2049*, the sequel, neon billboards flicker interchangeably in Japanese and Korean, villains wear deconstructed kimonos, but with the exception of a manicurist, there is no Asian soul in sight. We have finally vanished. The slaves, like Ryan Gosling, are all beautiful white replicants. The orphanage is full of young white boys who dismantle junked circuit boards, a scene taken straight out of present-day Delhi, where

Indian child laborers break down mountains of electronic waste while being poisoned by mercury toxins. *Blade Runner 2049* is an example of science fiction as magical thinking: whites fear that all the sins they committed against black and brown people will come back to them tenfold, so they fantasize their own fall as a preventative measure to ensure that the white race will never fall.

20

L for Lai Teck
by Ho Tzu Nyen

A fleet of illegible and nameless specters haunts
the political landscapes of early and mid-
twentieth-century Southeast Asia. British Special
Branch reports from this period tended to present its Communist enemies as faceless statistical
digits, revealing few personal details about
them. The abstraction of these reports is further
exacerbated by the fact that the most frequent
sources of intelligence were agents, double
agents, double-crossers, informers, snitches,
squealers, stool-pigeons, rats, spies, traitors,
tattletales, turncoats, and apostates—all of whom
have been known to fabricate stories.

This problem is symmetrically compounded
by the highly secretive and conspiratorial
nature of the Malayan Communist Party, which
bordered on the paranoid. Party statements
scarcely mentioned names, especially those of
their leaders and agents. This security measure
for concealing the identities of its operatives
seldom worked out in the longterm, and its
chief weakness was that it rendered these figures

invisible to the public, which had no image of the party's leadership or knowledge of its policies and activities.

From 1939 to 1947, the secretary general of the Malayan Communist Party was a man known as Lai Teck, sometimes written as Loi Tak, Lai Te, or Lai Rac as he was known to some in Vietnam. It has been said that he lived as Truong Phuoc Dat until 1934, but other sources report his birth name to be Nguyen Van Long, Hoang A Nhac, or Pham Van Dac. Throughout his career, Lai Teck accumulated more than fifty names: Lai Te, Lighter, Mr Light, Mr Wright, C.H. Chang, Chan Hung Chang, Chan Hoon, Chang Hung, Soh King, Lao Wu, Lee Soong, Wong Kim Geok, Huang Shao-dong, Jin Tang, D. Ling, the right hand of Ho Chih-Minh, Ah Le, Ah Lin, of Malaya's Lenin. He is every name in history. And in May 1948, the Central Committee of the Malayan Communist Party named him: "The greatest traitor in the history of our Party."

While there seems to be a consensus that he was born in 1903, accounts vary on his birthplace, which ranges from the Nghe Tinh Province of Vietnam to Saigon to Ba Ria in the south. But all commentators seem to agree that he was of mixed blood—with a Chinese

mother and an Annamese father—as though
this mélange prefigured the form, or rather, the
formlessness of his life.

Drawn to Communism at an early age, he
joined the Indochina Communist Party while
he was still a student in Saigon. After leaving
school, he entered the French Navy and lived a
life of water, circulating through the underbellies
of Asian port cities, among an interregional
cast of transients, seedy outlaws, and small-time
revolutionaries. For a person gifted with strong
mimetic faculties, life out in the open, fluid sea
was a constant temptation toward dissolution,
a slow unbounding of the self. For someone
like Lai Tek, to be at sea was to become sea, to
become water, in water.

In 1925, he was arrested by the French
Sûreté Générale Indochinoise for disseminating
Communist literature among sailors. Some
believe this to be the moment when he "turned"
to the other side; he would have been only
twenty-two years old. Others think that the turning point took place six years later, when he was
arrested at the French Concession in Shanghai.
In any case, Lai Teck worked in Vietnam as an
informer until 1934, when his cover was blown
in an incident in Annam. No longer useful to
French intelligence, he was gifted to the British,

with whom he would begin a new chapter
in his career. Authenticated by documents
that the Special Branch had seized in raids in
Hong Kong and Shanghai, Lai Teck arrived in
Singapore in 1934 with impressive credentials.
The British slyly cast him as a former aide of
Ho Chi Minh, which was convenient, given that
Ho had been arrested in Hong Kong in 1932.
Lai Teck arrived as a Comintern agent specially
sent to resolve an internal rift that was paralyz-
ing the Malayan Communist Party.

According to a Japanese military report
that surfaced after the war, "Comrade Wright"
made an immediate impression within the party.
His knowledge of theoretical Marxism earned
him the epithet of "Malaya's Lenin," while his
natural ability for organized destruction showed
itself in an intensive, six-month purge that
restored "ideological unity within the party."
Using the police to remove his competition,
he rapidly rose within the ranks of the party,
becoming secretary general in 1939.

When Singapore fell into Japanese hands
in February 1942, Lai Teck did not take to the
jungle like many of his comrades. He chose to
remain in the occupied city, according to one
source, accompanied by two Vietnamese wives
and a Chinese mistress, until he was picked up

by the Kempeitai in a security sweep. From then on, Lai Tek began working for the Japanese. News of his arrest spread, but so great was his aura within the party that it was believed that this master of espionage talked his way out of prison. In the years of the Japanese Occupation, Lai Teck went about his business flamboyantly, in a Morris Eight saloon given to him by the Japanese. But there can be little doubt that he facilitated the extensive destruction of the party's organization in Singapore and Malaya, often by setting up high-ranking party members for Kempeitai ambushes. Throughout his career, he was responsible for the arrest and execution of at least 105 party colleagues.

With the Japanese surrender and the return of Malaya to British rule, Lai Teck, with characteristic seamlessness, resumed his work with the British. However, suspicions against him had been accumulating in the last years of the war, and the Central Committee of the Party summoned Lai Tek for a meeting on March 6, 1947. Sensing that something was amiss, Lai Teck did not turn up. Instead, he spent the next months in hiding before disappearing with most of the party's funds to Hong Kong. However, prior to this, Lai Teck had made what was arguably his most far-reaching political move—steering the armed, anti-Japanese Communist guerillas away from a forceful takeover of Malaya before the British return. And when Chin Peng, who succeeded Lai Teck as secretary general in 1947, led the party to armed struggle, the initiative had already been lost. Vessel to every power, in the vicissitudes of Lai Teck's career, can be traced a chronicle of the entire region's political turmoil.

The death of Lai Teck, like so much of his life, came through hearsay. According to Chin Peng, whose account was in itself the result of a sequence of Chinese whispers, Lai Teck was tracked down in Thailand in 1947 by a death squad. He was suffocated, his body stuffed in a sack, and thrown into the Chao Phraya River. A watery grave for a man whose being in the world was like water in water.

The closest thing to an official confirmation of Lai Teck's death is the recent release of his picture by the Special Branch, something that is usually done upon the death of former agents. In this single photograph of him that survives, we see a lean and severe man with large, deep-set eyes staring straight out at us. Cloaked in blankness, this is a face that lends itself easily to our imaginative projections of cloak-and-dagger fantasies. And in the very inconsistency of his soul, we sense an incompleteness that defines the region as a whole; an identity not defined by interiority of substance, but shaped through exteriority and regionality. In the uncertain and ambiguous biography of this nameless shape-shifter is inscribed the history of Southeast Asia: subjected to multiple possessions and manifold dominations, alongside a brute—and mute—will to survive.

Sketches
by Tishan Hsu

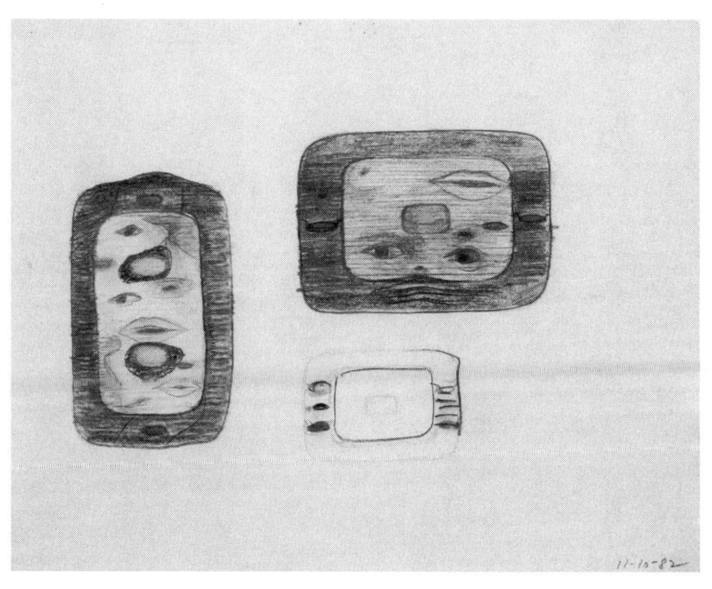

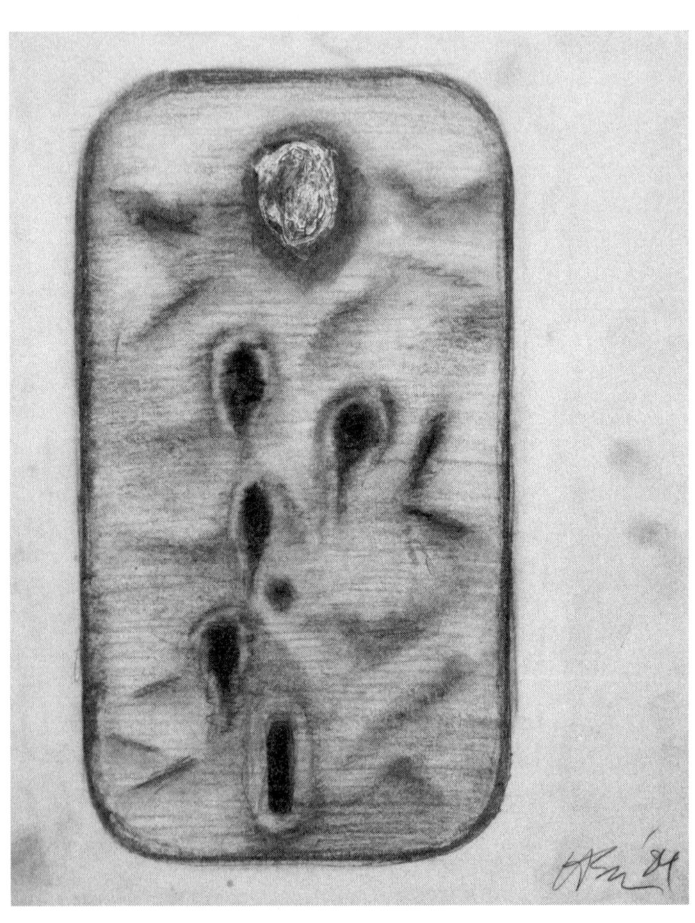

178

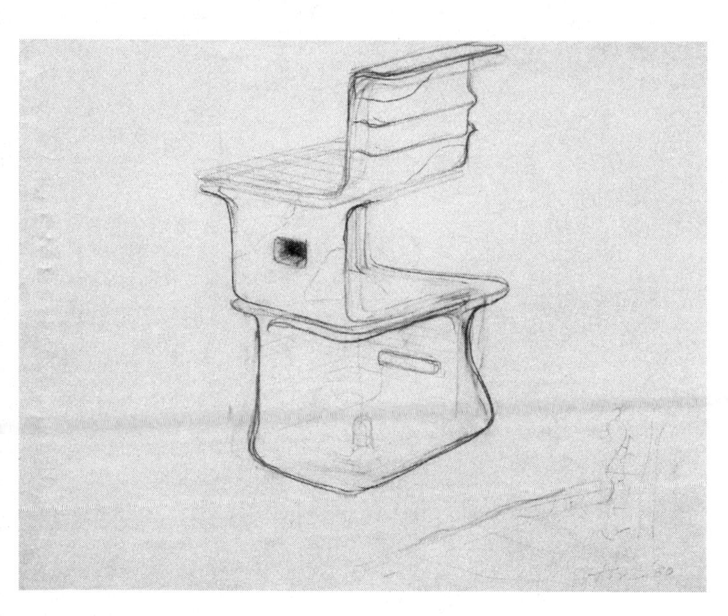

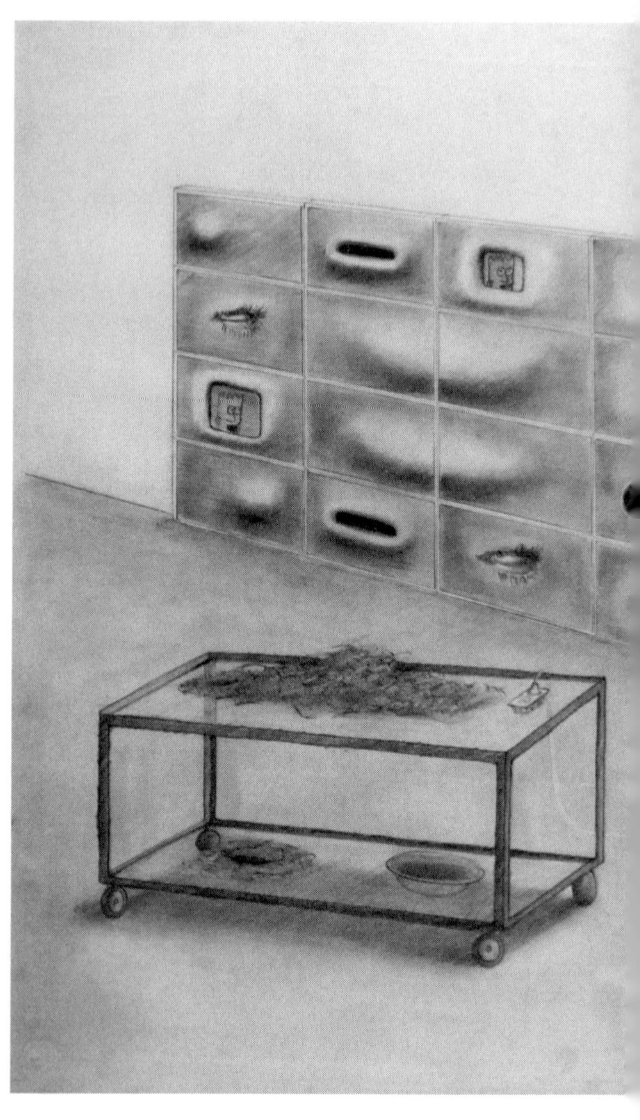

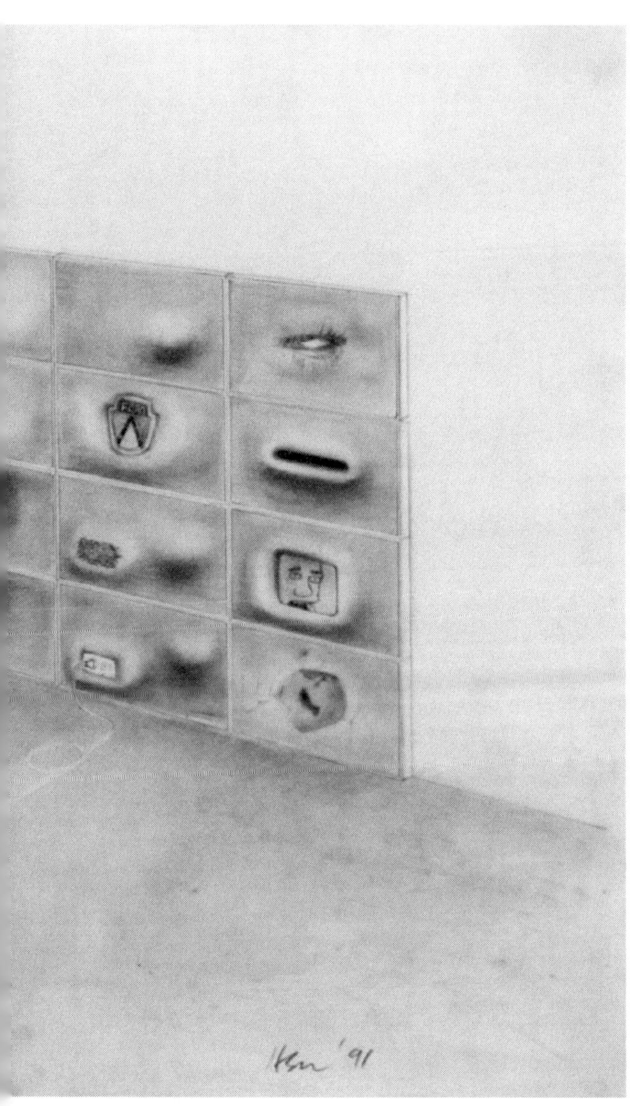

Ksr '91

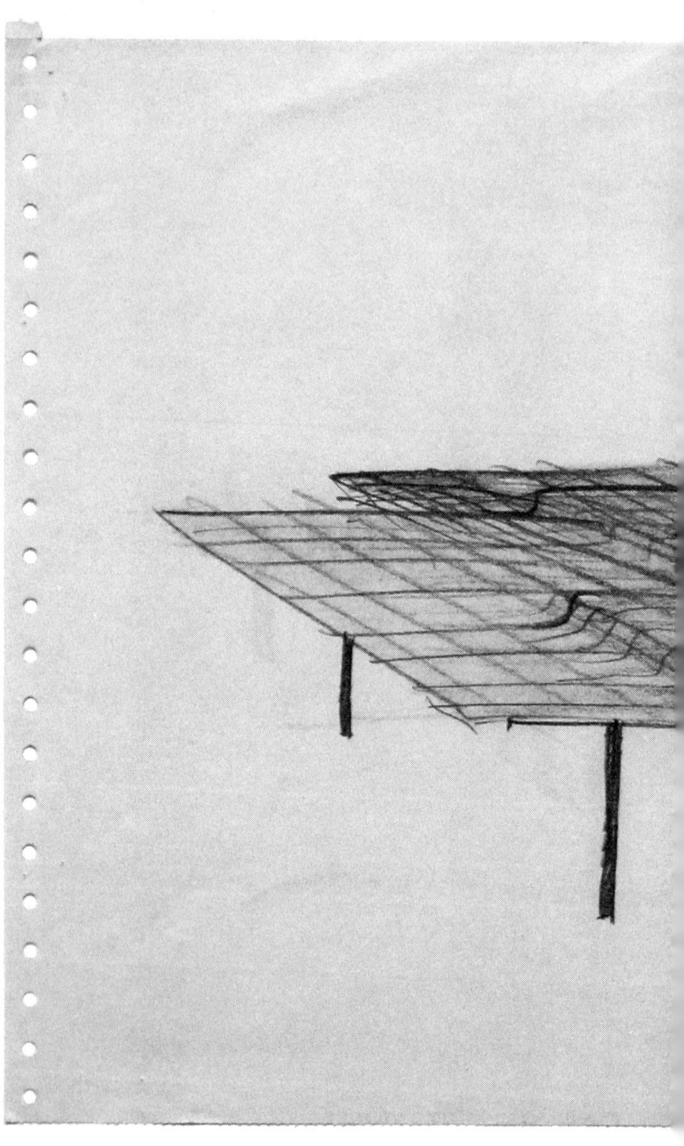

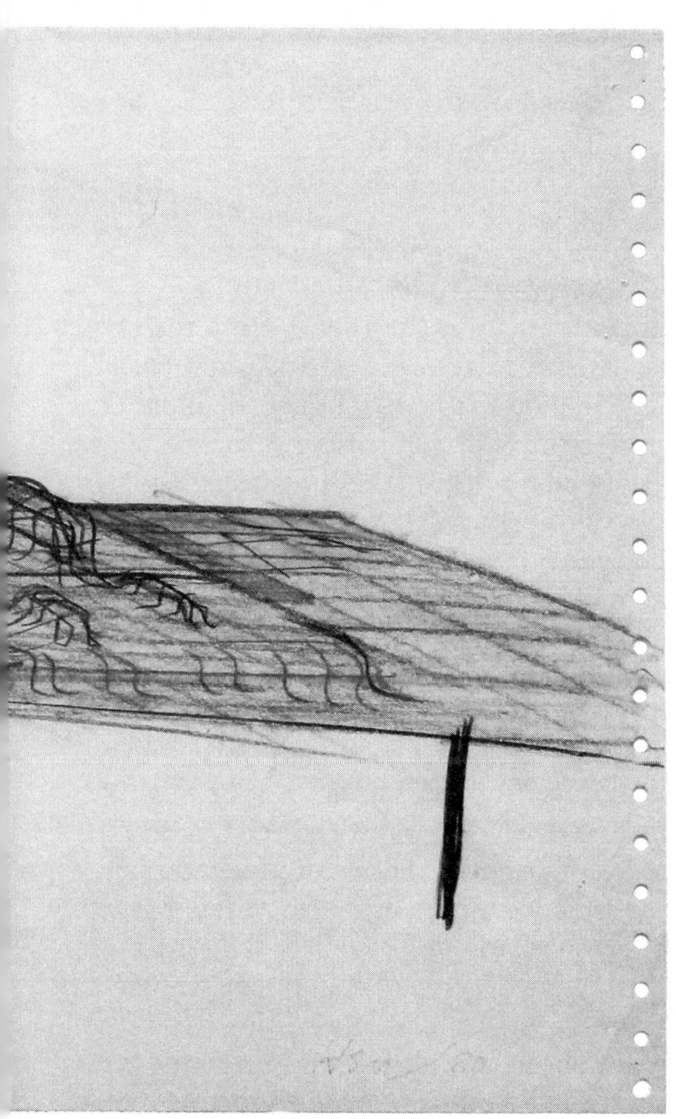

22

Toxic Worlding
by Mel Y. Chen

Recall that matters of life and death have arguably underlain queer theory from the early 1990s, when radical queer activism in relation to AIDS blended saliently with academic theorizing on politics of gender and sexuality. More recently, Lee Edelman takes up a psychoanalytic analysis of queerness's figural deathly assignment in relation to a relentless "reproductive futurism."[1] Jasbir Puar points to life and death economies that place some queer subjects in the privileged realm of a biopolitically "optimized life," while other perverse subjects are consigned to the realm of death, as a "result of the successes of queer incorporation into the domains of consumer markets and social recognition in the post-civil rights, late twentieth century."[2] Similar affective pulses of surging lifeliness or morbid resignation might reflect the legacy of the deathly impact of AIDS in queer scholarship. Suggesting a "horizontal" imagining whose terms are pointedly not foretold by a pragmatic limitation on the present, José Esteban Muñoz in *Cruising Utopia* offers a way around the false promise of a neoliberal, homonormative utopia whose major concerns are limited to gay marriage and gay service in the military: lifely for a few, deathly for others.[3]

To enact a method that prioritizes a queer reach for toxicity's "worlding," I want to interleave considerations of toxicity and intoxication with a "toxic sensorium": a sense memory of objects and affects that was my felt orientation to the world when I was recently categorized as "ill." It seems never a simple matter to discuss toxicity, to objectify it. It is yet another matter to experience something that seems by one measure or another to be categorized as a toxin, to undergo intoxication, intoxification. This difference raises questions about toxic methodology, which in some way inherits anthropology's question about what can be done to respond to crises of objectivity. While no simple solution exists, it is my interest to attenuate the exceptionalisms that attain all too easily in, for instance, the previous chapter's assessment of lead toxicity's discursive range: it is possible for a reader to comfortably reside in a certain sense of integral, nontoxic security in that analysis.

To intensify toxicity's intuitive reach, I engage toxicity as a *condition*, one that is too

complex to imagine as a property of one or
another individual or group or something that
could itself be so easily bounded. I would like to
deemphasize the borders of the immune system
and its concomitant attachments to "life" and
"death," such that the immune system's aim is to
realize and protect life. How can we think more
broadly about synthesis and symbiosis, including
toxic vapors, interspersals, intrinsic mixings,
and alterations, favoring interabsorption over
corporeal exceptionalism? I will not address these
questions from a point of view of mythic health.
Rather, I will tell a tale from the perspective of
the existence that I have recently claimed, one
that has been quite accurately considered "toxic."

In other words, I move now from a theoretical discussion of metaphors about threat
into what feels, for me personally, like riskier
terrain, the terrain of the autobiographical. As
academics are often trained to avoid writing in
anything resembling a confessional mode, such
a turn is fraught with ambivalence. I theorize
toxicity as it has profoundly impacted my own
health, my own queerness, and my own ability to
forge bonds, and in so doing, I offer a means to
reapproach questions of animacy with a different
lens. This theorization through the "personal"
is not intended as a perfect subjectivity that

opposes an idealized objectivity. Rather, it is meant as a complementary kind of knowledge production, one that in this context invites both the sympathetic ingestion (or intoxication) of what remains a marked experience, and the empathetic memory of past association. It centers on a set of states and experiences that have been diagnosed as "multiple chemical sensitivity" and "heavy metal poisoning," and can be used to think more deeply about this condition and what it offers to thinking about bodies and affect. As such, my repository of thoughts, experiences, and theorizations while ill—ones that queerly and profoundly changed my relationship to intimacy—could be considered a kind of "archive of feelings,'" to use Ann Cvetkovich's important terminology.[4] These are feelings that are neither exclusively traumatic, nor exclusively private, nor a social archive proper to certain groups: they are feelings whose publics and intimacies are not clearly bounded or determinable. Such feelings—and their intimacies—offer a way to come at normative affect's margins. Where Lauren Berlant notes, of less institutionalized interactions, that "intimacy names the enigma of this range of attachments ... and it poses a question of scale that links the instability of individual lives to the trajectories of the collective," I mean to destabilize where the toxic and its affects can be located.[5]

I have for the last few years suffered from the effects of mercury toxicity, perhaps related to receiving for a decade in my childhood weekly allergy shots which were preserved with mercury, and having a mouth full of "metal" fillings which were composed of mercury amalgam. That said, I am not invested in tracing or even asserting a certain cause and effect of my intoxication, not least because such an endeavor would require its own science studies of Western medicine's ambivalent materialization of heavy metal intoxication as an identifiable health concern. Rather, I wish to chart such intoxications with and against sexuality, as both of these are treated as biologized and cultural forms with specific ethical politics. In early twenty-first century US culture, queer subjects are in many ways treated as toxic assets, participating in the flow of capital as a new niche market, yet also threatening to dismantle marriage or infiltrate the military, and thus potentially damaging the very economic and moral stability of the nation. But what happens when queers become intoxicated? Recall the earlier secondary *Oxford English Dictionary* meanings of *queer* as both "unwell" and "drunk," the latter of which is now proclaimed to be obsolete; such meanings shadow queerness with the cast of both illness and inebriation. While Muñoz meditates on the possibilities of ecstasy—the drug—as a metaphor for pleasurable queer temporalities,[6] I explore an intoxication that is not voluntary, is potentially permanent, is ambivalent toward its own affective uptake, and produces an altered affect that may not register its own pleasure or negativity in recognizable terms.

Let me get specific and narrate what my "toxic" cognitive and bodily state means, how it limits, delimits, frames, and undoes. Today I am having a day of relative wellbeing and am eager to explore my neighborhood on foot; I have forgotten for the moment that I just don't go places "on foot," because the results can be catastrophic. Having moved to a new place, with the fresh and heady defamiliarization that comes with uprooting and replanting, my body has forgotten some of its belabored environmental repertoire, its micronarratives of movement and response, of engagement and return, of provocation and injury. It is for a moment free—in its scriptless version of its future—to return to former ways of inhabiting space when I was in better health. Some passenger cars whiz by; instinctively my body retracts and my corporeal-sensory vocabulary starts to kick back in. A few pedestrians cross my path, and before they near, I quickly assess whether they are likely (or might be the "kind of people") to wear perfumes or colognes or to be wearing sunscreen. I scan their head for smoke puffs or pursed lips pre-release; I scan their hands for a long white object, even a stub. In an instant, quicker than I thought anything could reach my organs, my liver refuses to process these inhalations and screams hate, a hate whose intensity each time shocks me.

I am accustomed to this; the glancing scans kick in from habit whenever I am witnessing proximate human movement, and I have learned to prepare to be disappointed. This preparation for disappointment is something like the preparation for the feeling I would get as a young person when I looked, however glancingly, into the eyes of a racist passerby who expressed apparent disgust at my Asian off-gendered form. I imagined myself as the queer child who was simultaneously a walking piece of dirt from Chinatown. For the sake of survival, I now have a strategy of temporally displaced imaginations; if my future includes places and people, I pattern-match them to past experiences with chemically similar places and chemically similar

people. I run through the script to see if it would
result in continuity or discontinuity. This system
of simultaneous conditionals and the time-space
planning that results runs counter to my other
practice for survival, an investment in a refusal
of conditions for my existence, a rejection
of a history of racial tuning and internalized
vigilance.

To my relief, the pedestrians pass, unevent-
fully for my body. I realize then that I should
have taken my chemical respirator with me.
When I used to walk maskless with unsuspecting
acquaintances, they had no idea that I was
privately enacting my own bodily concert of
breath-holding, speech, and movement; that
while concentrating on the topic of conversation, I was also highly alert to our environment
and still affecting full involvement by limiting
movements of my head while I scanned.
Sometimes I had no breath stored and had to
scoot ahead to a clearer zone while explaining
hastily "I can't do the smoke." Indeed, the
grammatical responsibility is clear here: the
apologetic emphasis is always on I-statements
because there is more shame and implicature
(the implicit demand for my interlocutor to
do something about it) in "the smoke makes
me sick," so I avoid it. Yet the individuated

property-assignation of "I am highly sensitive"
furthers the fiction of my dependence as against
others' independence. The question then
becomes which bodies can bear the fiction of
independence and uninterruptability.

I am, in fact still seeking ways to effect a smile
behind my mask: lightening my tone, cracking
jokes, making small talk about the weather, or
simply surging forward with whatever energy I
have to connect with a person on loving terms.
I did this recently when I had to go with a mask
into Michael's crafts shop, full as it is of scents
and glues and fiberboard. The register clerk was
very sweet, very friendly, and to my relief did
not consider the site of intersubjectivity to be
the two prominent chemical filter discs on either
side of my mask. "Wearing the mask with love" is
the same way I learned to deal with a rare racial
appearance in my white-dominated hometown
in the Midwest, or with what is read as a transna-
tionally gendered ambiguity. It seems the result I
receive in return is either love or hostility, and it
is unpredictable. Suited up in both racial skin and
chemical mask, I am perceived as a walking symbol of a contagious disease like SARS, and am
often met with some form of repulsion; indeed,
"SARS!" is what has been used to interpellate me
in the streets.

As many thinkers have noted, the insinuation or revelation of a disability, particularly invisible disability, dovetails interestingly with issues of coming-out discourses of sexuality and passing. Both Ellen Samuels and Robert McRuer have discussed the ways in which "coming out" as disabled provocatively overlaps with, and also differs from, "coming out" as queer.[7] How does a mask help interrupt the notion of "passing"? How does it render as "damaged" (or, at least, vulnerable) a body that might otherwise seem healthy? Not wearing a chemical mask counts as a guise of passing, of the appearance of non-disability: I look "well" when I am maskless in public, at least until I crumple.

The use of the literal mask as an essential prosthesis for environmentally ill subjects is notable in light of Tobin Siebers's deployment of "masquerade" as an *exaggeration* of disability symbols to manage or intervene in social schemas about ability and disability.[8] This dialogic friction between actual mask as facial appurtenance—the mask's literal locus on the face—and mask or masquerade as a racial, nondisabled, or sexuality *metaphor* points to the central significance of face as intersubjective locus, and it exemplifies the expropriability of a facial notion of embattlement to the rest of the (human) body or to social spheres of interaction;[9] but it also points to the complexities that emerge when the actual facial signification of disability rubs up against the facial mask metaphor. Arguably, a chemical mask can serve as its own masquerade, but it also slips and slides into orthogonal significations. Its reading as *exaggeration*, in particular, competes with its reading as racializing and masculinizing toxic *threat*, where the skin of the mask ambivalently locates the threat on either side of it. The same ambivalence may be attributed to the "skins" of some toxic bodies, whereas synecdochal attribution of toxicity applies either to the (rest of the) toxic body itself (the mask standing for the human SARS vector) or to an exterior, vulnerable body that renders it so (Frantz Fanon's "skin," which the "mask" covers, standing in for the colonial racialized visualities that render his blackness toxic to a white collective).[10] Is, then, the toxic body the disabled body? Or is the toxic body that collective body that biopolitically inoculates itself against a stronger toxin by affording itself homeopathic amounts of a "negative" toxin (disabled bodies) while remaining in a terrible tension with these negated entities?

Given my condition, I must constantly renegotiate, and recalibrate, my embodied experiences of intimacy, altered affect, and the

porousness of the body. The nature of metal
poisoning, accumulated over decades, is that
any and every organ, including my brain, can
bear damage. Because symptoms can reflect the
toxicity of any organ, they form a laundry list
that includes cognition, proprioception, emotion,
agitation, muscle strength, tunnel perception,
joint pain, and nocturnality. Metal-borne damage
to the liver's detoxification pathways means that
I cannot sustain many everyday toxins: once they
enter, they recirculate rather than leave. I can
sometimes become "autism-spectrum" in the
sense that I cannot take too much stimulation,
including touch, sound, or direct human engagement, including being unable to meet someone's
gaze, needing repetitive, spastic movements to
feel that my body is just barely in a tolerable
state; and I can radically lose compassionate
intuition, saying things that I feel innocuous but
are incredibly hurtful. The word *mercurial* means
what it means—unstable and wildly unpredictable—because the mercury toxin has altered a
self, has directly transformed an effective matrix:
affect goes faster, affect goes hostile, goes toxic.
Traditional psychology here, I suspect, can
only be an overlay, a reading of what has already
transformed the body; it cannot fully rely on
its narratives.

Largely two quarters of the animated agents of the metropolis—that is, motor vehicles and pedestrians, but not the nonhuman animals or the insects—can be toxic to me because they are proximate instigators. The smokestacks, though they set the ambient tone of the environment, are of less immediate concern when I am surviving moment to moment. Efficiency is far from my aim; that would mean traversing the main streets. Because I must follow the moment-to-moment changes in quality of air to inhale something that won't hurt me, turning toward a thing or away from it correspondingly, humans are to a radical degree no longer the primary cursors of my physical inhabitation of space. Inanimate things take on a greater, holistic importance. It also means that I am perpetually itinerant, even when I have a goal; it means I will never walk in a straight line. There are also lessons here, reminders of interdependency, of softness, of fluidity, of receptivity, of immunity's fictivity and attachment's impermanence; life sustains even—or especially—in this kind of silence, this kind of pause, this dis-ability. The heart pumps blood; the mind, even when it says, "I can't think," has reflected where and how it *is*. Communion is possible in spite of, or even because of, this fact.

To conclude this narration of a day navigating my own particular hazards: I've made it back home and lie on the couch, and I won't be able to rise. My lover comes home and greets me; I grunt a facsimile of greeting in return, looking only in her general direction but not into her eyes. She comes near to offer comfort, putting her hand on my arm, and I flinch away; I can't look at her and hardly speak to her; I can't recall words when I do. She tolerates this because she understands very deeply how I am toxic. What is this relating? Distance in the home becomes the condition of these humans living together in this moment, humans who are geared not toward continuity or productivity or reproductivity but to stasis, to waiting, until it passes.

In such a toxic period, anyone or anything that I manage to feel any kind of connection with, whether it's my cat or a chair or a friend or a plant or a stranger or my partner, I think they are, and remember they are, all the same ontological thing. What happens to notions of animacy given this lack of distinction between "living" and "lifely" things? I am shocked when my lover doesn't remember what I told "her" about my phone earlier that day, when it was actually a customer service representative on a chat page, which once again brings an animating transitivity into play. And I am shocked when her body does not reflect that I have snuggled against it earlier, when the snuggling and comforting happened in the arm and back of my couch. What body am I now in the arms of? Have I performed the inexcusable: Have I treated my girlfriend like my couch? Or have I treated my couch like her, which fares only slightly better in the moral equations? Or have I done neither such thing? After I recover, the conflation seems unbelievable. But it is only in the recovering of my human-directed sociality that the couch really becomes an unacceptable partner. This episode, which occurs again and again, forces me to rethink animacy, since I have encountered an intimacy that does not differentiate, is not dependent on a heartbeat. The couch and I are interabsorbent, interporous, and not only because the couch is made of mammalian skin. These are intimacies that are often ephemeral, and they are lively; and I wonder whether or how much they are really made of habit.

Notes

1   Lee Edelman, *No Future: Queer Theory and the Death Drive* (Duke University Press, 2004), 2.
2   Jasbir K. Puar, *Terrorist Assemblages: Homonationalism in Queer Times* (Duke University Press, 2007).
3   José Esteban Muñoz, *Cruising Utopia: The Then and There of Queer Futurity* (NYU Press, 2009).
4   Ann Cvetkovich, *An Archive of Feelings: Trauma, Sexuality, and Lesbian Public Cultures* (Duke University Press, 2003).
5   Lauren Berlant, "Intimacy: A Special Issue," *Critical Inquiry* 24, no. 2 (Winter 1998): 281–88.
6   Muñoz, *Cruising Utopia*, 185–89.
7   For complexities of passing and disclosure, see Ellen Samuels, "My Body, My Closet" in GLQ: A Journal of Lesbian and Gay Studies, Duke University Press, vol. 9, no. 1–2, 2003, 233–55; and Robert McRuer's chapter "Coming Out Crip" in *Crip Theory* (NYU Press, 2006), 33–76.
8   Tobin Siebers, *Disability Theory* (University of Michigan Press, 2008), 101-8. On compulsory able-bodiedness in relation to queer-crip

perspectives, see McRuer, *Crip Theory*; Alison Kafer, "Compulsory Bodies," Journal of Women's History, Johns Hopkins University Press, Vol. 15, No. 3, Autumn 2003, 77-89; Eli Clare, *Exile and Pride* (Duke University Press, 1999).

9   The sociologist Erving Goffman's *Stigma* considers visible disability, particularly disfigurement, as a kind of social stigma and the ways in which it is managed in conversation.

10 I am texturing an analysis of toxicity here to consider negatively racialized bodies as themselves "toxic bodies." See, for instance, the oft-cited scene from Frantz Fanon's *Black Skin, White Masks*, in which the narrator considers his racialized objectification by a white child and by other whites.

23

INITIAL PUBLIC OFFERING OOOO (IPOOOOO)
by Jen Liu

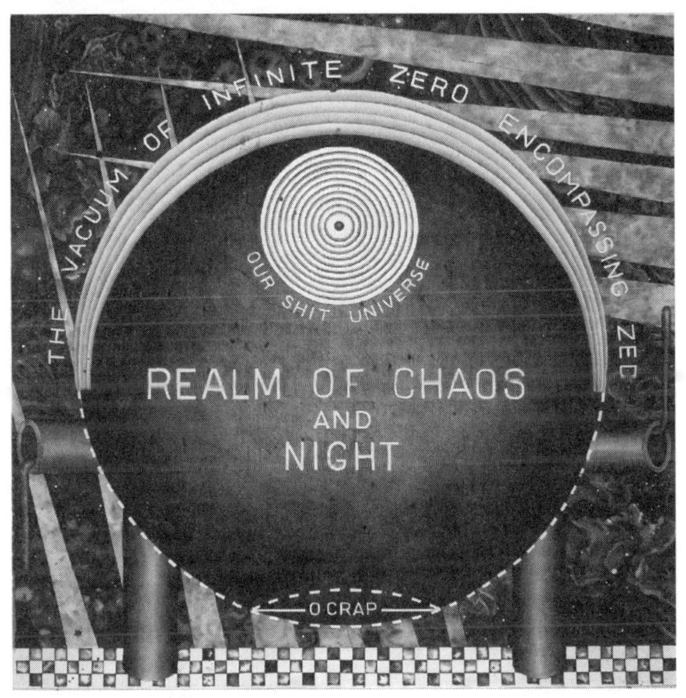

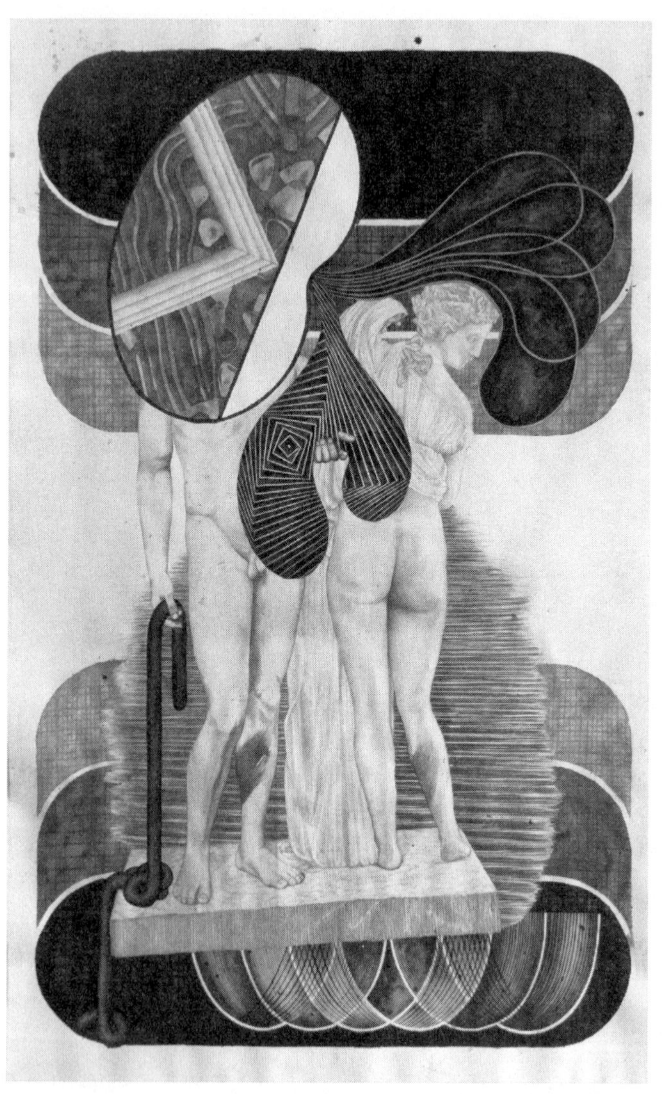

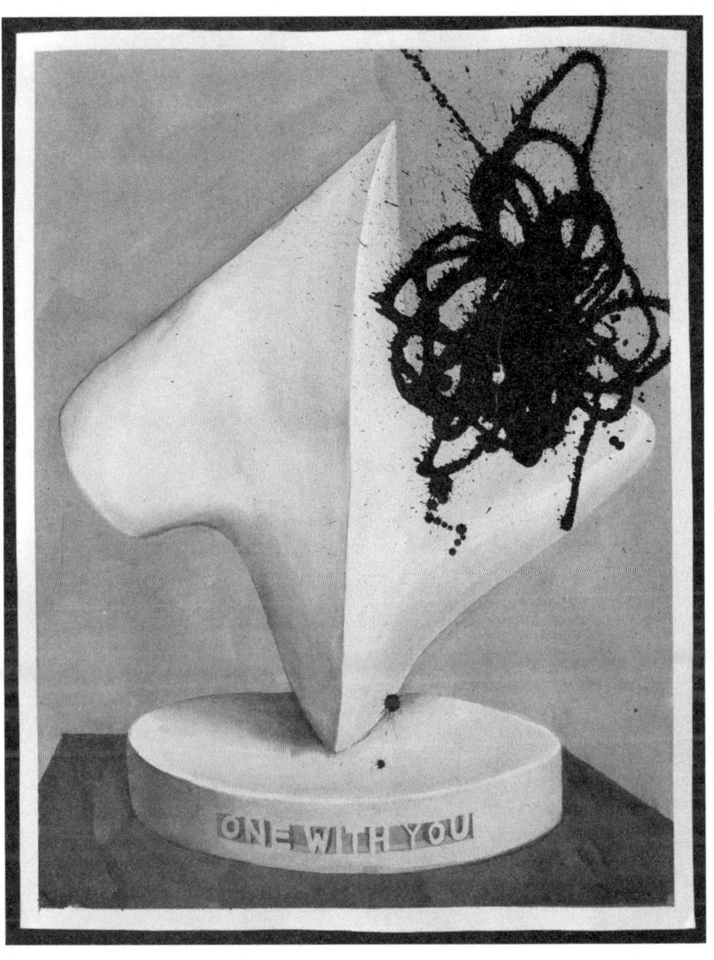
ONE WITH YOU

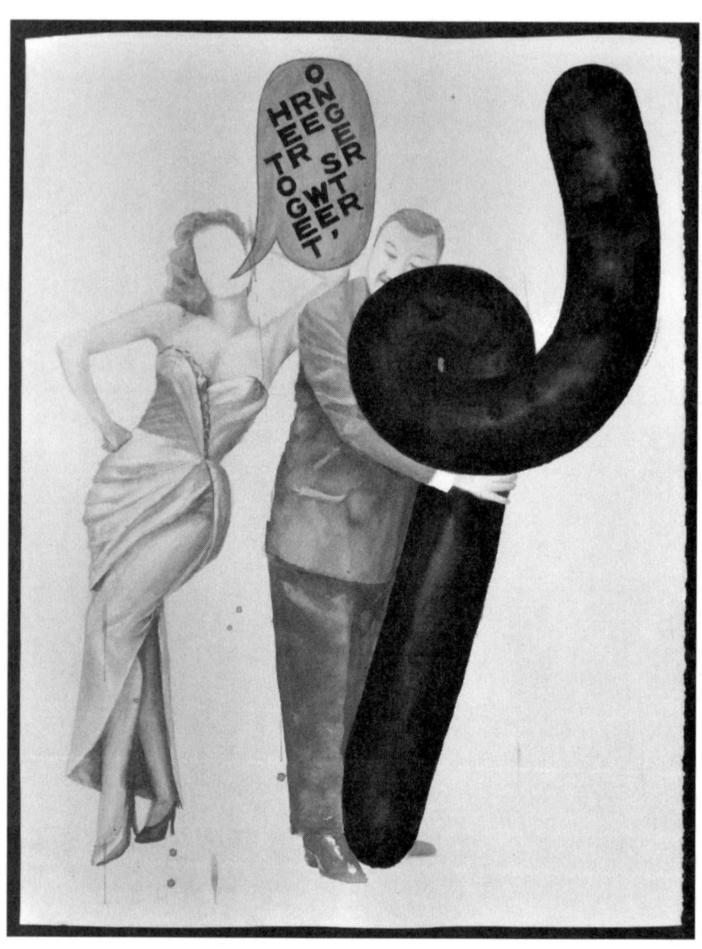

O N
H R G
E E E
E R S R
T O W T
G E E R
E E
T ,

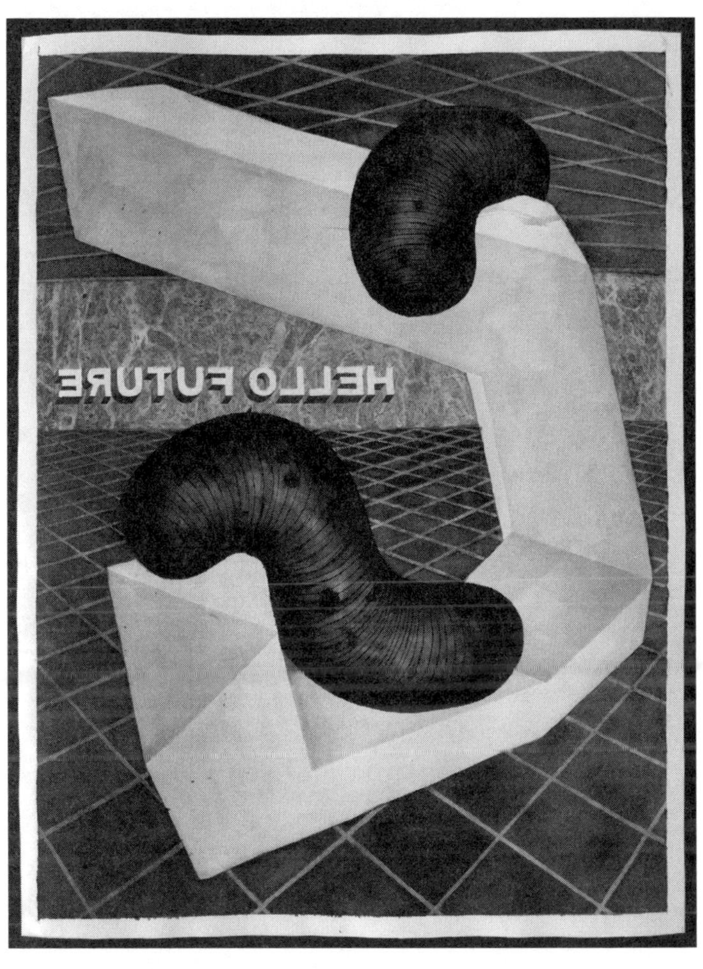
HELLO FUTURE

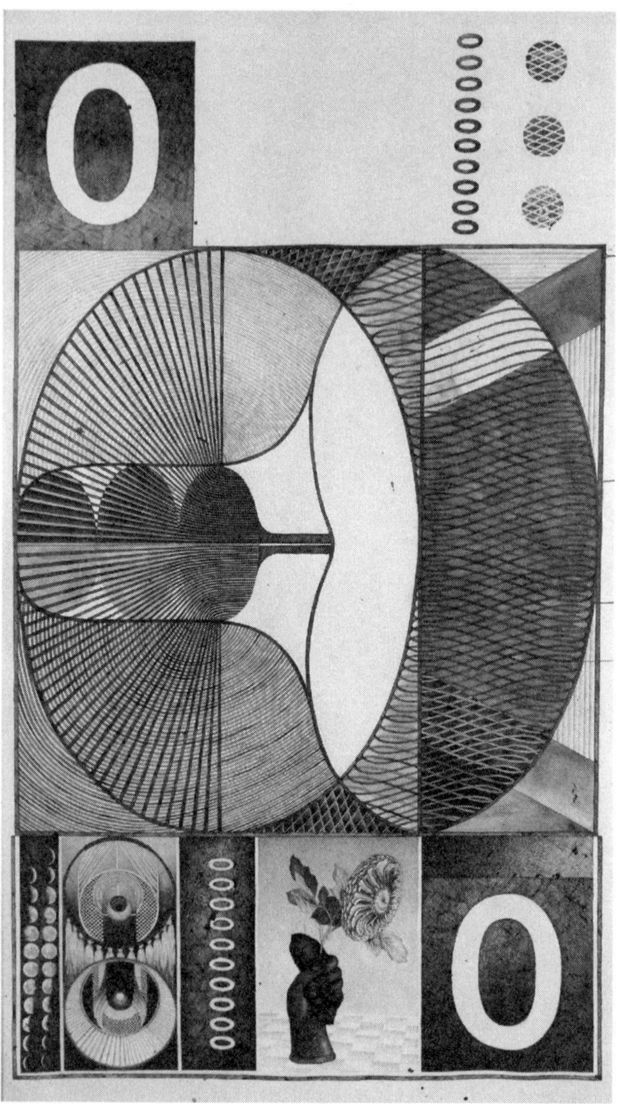

Symbiontics: a view of present conditions from a place of entanglement
by Caroline A. Jones

The specifics demanded of pandemical philosophy call up the paradox of connection at a distance. *Connection* forged by the act of communication across a few feet of air, that can nonetheless vector thousands of virions, expelled from the breath of a single speaker.[1] (These are the unwitting microbial aggressions that connect us as linked vectors of a pathogen.) *Connection* across antagonistic lines, as bodies classed and raced by governmentality are literally (op)pressed by other bodies deposed to govern them with intimate, grinding, daily violence. (These are the witting macro- and micro-aggressions that connect us via the flexible ligaments of divisive racism.) *Connection*, even for those attempting to break connections and isolate, or connect in anti-racism, in our humming social media.

These are new positions for many, if familiar to some—displaced, out of place, replaced. By shifting orientations—intentionally deforming the "straight" lines bodies are supposed to take, analyzing the places we are now meant to stay in (our) place. It requires a detouring from the normativizing socius, a *standing with*—connecting by turning away (to form a newer kind of together). Sara Ahmed is a superlative guide to these necessary displacements. The aim is to yield a new philosophy of connection and orientation that opens onto the "difficulty" of difference (and, I will argue here, the symbiosis of our with-living). Ahmed starts with phenomenology:

> I start *here* because phenomenology makes "orientation" central in the very argument that consciousness is always directed "toward" an object, and given its emphasis on the lived experience of inhabiting a body, or what Edmund Husserl calls the "living body" *(Leib)*. […] The attribution of feeling toward an object (I feel afraid because you are fearsome) moves the subject away from the object, creating distance through the registering of proximity as a threat.[2]

Recognizing fear as a *spatial affect* (proximity as threat), Ahmed's queer phenomenology is a precious resource for those of us who work in culture, or teach in architecture schools, or feel afraid. In the time of the novel coronavirus, the *threat* posed by proximity takes on multiple meanings, since the pandemic amplifies every privilege and every inequity a hundred-fold. This amplification, an effect of the multiplied crises produced by bad government, brings biological systems and political philosophies much closer together. This becomes another turning, connecting across disciplinary distance as well as among micro- macro-scales. Useful here is the renegade second-order cybernetics of Heinz von Foerster (the physicist and philosopher who found useful the precepts of "Uncle Ludwig" Wittgenstein, who also got the heck out of Vienna during the rise of fascism).[3]

Von Foerster played a major role in what Margaret Mead called the "cybernetics of cybernetics"—the move in systems theory to begin to understand how the observer's *having* a systems theory would demand that the observer would now have to become a feature in their own analysis of whatever system they observed. This crucial move jibed both with theories of the smallest scale (quantum entanglement), and observations of the largest.[4] In sum, von Foerster contributed theoretically to the understanding that there are always nested systems, all the way down and all the way up, confounding the "black box" of engineering with a new science of complexity. These neo-cybernetic concepts also fed the growing realization that the Earth's atmosphere was being maintained in its homeostasis (oxygen / carbon dioxide / nitrogen) by the life forms it harbored. The lowliest cyanobacteria had evolved to produce oxygen, which, in "poisoning" the atmosphere, pushed anaerobic entities into safer spaces and drove the evolution of oxygenating and respirating life forms with their novel reproductive modes (plants and animals).[5] Since this Great Oxygenation Event and its impact on evolution, life itself has maintained the system's balance of carbon and oxygen, with the happenstance of a planetary magnetic core holding radiation at bay and gravity keeping that atmosphere around.

Thinking of earth-systems and microbial-systems at the same time required a more-than-human phenomenology that extended, in von Foerster's thinking, from the basic apprehension of a world to the way its information might be organized against entropy. "We can understand things only by handling them, by moving them, by moving our own body…," yet if our very understanding happens phenomenologically, in that *Leib* or living body, we can nonetheless extend our haptic way of knowing inductively to conceptualize all the systems in which

we are nested. In this, von Foerster applied
Wittgenstein's logic of induction, seeing ways in
which that dry mathematization could inform
the burgeoning cybernetic discourse around
life systems. These were in the process of being
galvanized in the late '50s by theories of "self-
organizing systems," which would be dubbed, by
Latin American biologists Humberto Maturana
and Francisco Varela, *autopoiesis* ("poiesis" added
to "auto" or self, for self-*creating* systems). So
even if "you need the motorium to understand
the sensorium," von Foerster showed how we
can use logic to think through the organizing
complexity of the universe and the negentropic
life that manifestly blooms within it.[6]

On the one hand, von Foerster wanted
to resist the suddenly hip terminology of
"self-organizing systems," as this implied
closed autonomous entities (perhaps with
neither "motorium" or "sensorium") that
would directly confound the second law of
thermodynamics. (Any closed system, he argued,
is subject to grinding entropy.)[7] On the other,
his philosophical inclinations wanted to bring
life into these cybernetic loops—already hinted
by his courtship of phenomenology (Husserl's
Leib). In a crucial paper, "On Self-Organizing
Systems and Their Environments" from 1959,

he solves the dilemma, pointing out the illogic of "self-organizing" with a deft application of Uncle Ludwig's *Tractatus* proposition 6.31,[8] but then finding a way to save the phenomenon of *poiesis* by insisting on one system nesting within another:

> I propose to continue the use of the term "self-organizing system," whilst being aware of the fact that this term becomes meaningless, unless the system is in close contact with an environment, *which possesses available energy and order*, and with which our system is in a state of perpetual interaction, such that it somehow manages to "live" on the expenses of this environment.[9]

We now come to the neologism of my title, which requires me to break down for digestion that wet-but-crunchy term *symbiontics*.[10] The "ontic" ending takes a term from technical philosophy, a tiny seme at the heart of the vast project of "ontology"—the study of what is. *Symbiontics* embeds that notion of "what is," the ontic, with *symbiosis*, the condition of "with-living" that biologists began to identify under that word in the late nineteenth century.[11] Symbiontics asks that we retool phenomenology to move outside the limiting philosophy of the "individual," to capture the ever-expanding scales of our sym-poietic (not just *auto*poietic) systems.[12]

This is, as Ahmed recommends, a marked detouring or queering of the conventional obsession (conveyed by Western-style philosophy) with that singular construct we call an "individual," packaged within an envelope of skin or a brain-filled cranial cavity. Given what we now know about the gut brain and its dependence on cultivated xenobacteria, or the plasma-based immune brain with its primordial system of chemical defenders and epigenetic recruitments for molecular learning (as from vaccines), it is clear that humans are never independent of the systems of matter and life on this planet—we are utterly entangled with them. In Karen Barad's compelling philosophy drawn from quantum theory, this point becomes characteristic of all observations, and all knowledge: we and our apparatuses are woven into how, and what, we know.[13]

This was the point of Heinz von Foerster's beautiful neo-cybernetic conundrum. We can fantasize the "self-organizing system" of the self, *as long as we maintain its status as both environmentally open and operationally closed.*[14] Thus we want the effect of clarifying wonder—experienced as miraculous in the glimmerings of understanding of true complexity—rather than the fetish magic of concealment that would give the embodied attribute of intelligence to our machines.[15] Pandemical philosophy demands *symbiontics*, a phenomenological grappling with entangled symbiosis and eco-logics, where connecting across distance is where we are, and what we do.

Notes

1 Caroline A. Jones, "Virions: Thinking through the Scale of Aggregation," *Artforum* 58, vol. 9 (May/June 2020): 98–101, 196.

2 Sara Ahmed, "Introduction," in *Queer Phenomenology: Orientations, Objects, Others* (Duke University Press, 2006), 2.

3 My account of Heinz von Foerster is deeply indebted to Bruce Clarke's exegesis of his ideas. See Clarke and Mark B. N. Hansen, eds., *Emergence and Embodiment: New Essays on Second-Order Systems Theory* (Duke University Press, 2009).

4 As a basic example: by setting up a mountaintop observatory that runs on energy generated by coal from miles away, one that produces noise in the grinding of its gears,

we must feature these facts of the apparatus in parsing the data: emissions change the atmosphere through which we are attempting to observe the distant universe, and sonic vibrations can deform the data we seek.

5   Lynn Sagan, "On the Origin of Mitosing Cells," *Journal of Theoretical Biology* 14 (1967): 225–74. After her divorce from Carl Sagan, Lynn (née Alexander, became Margulis) made common cause with James Lovelock in launching the Gaia theory, for which see James E. Lovelock and Lynn Margulis, "Atmospheric Homeostasis by and for the Biosphere: The Gaia Hypothesis," *Tellus* 26, issue 1–2 (1974): 1–10. For a recent compelling take, we await the forthcoming essay by Leah Aronowsky. "Gas Guzzling Gaia, or: A Prehistory of Climate Change Denialism." *Critical Inquiry* 47, no. 2 (2021): 306–27. https://doi.org/10.1086/712129.

6   Heinz von Foerster, in Clarke and Hansen, *Emergence and Embodiment*, 31.

7   For a view on the cultural impact of entropy see Jones, "Entropies," in *Energies in the Arts*, ed. Douglas Kahn (MIT Press, 2019), 263–307.

8   Ludwig Wittgenstein, *Tractatus Logico-Philosophicus*, trans. Charles Kay Ogden

(1922), online at https://en.wikisource.org
/wiki/Tractatus_Logico-Philosophicus/6.
Accessed June 4, 2020, proposition 6.31:
"The so-called law of induction cannot in
any case be a logical law, for it is obviously
a significant proposition.—And therefore it
cannot be a law a priori either." This follows
the trenchant precept "Outside logic all is
accident."

9   Heinz von Foerster, "On Self-Organizing
Systems and Their Environments,"
adaptation of an address given at The
Interdisciplinary Symposium on Self-
Organizing Systems, on May 5, 1959, in
Chicago, Illinois, and first published in
Self-Organizing Systems, M.C. Yovits and
S. Cameron, eds. (Pergamon Press, 1960),
31–50. The edition quoted here has been
anthologized in Foerster, *Understanding
Understanding*: *Essays on Cybernetics and
Cognition* (Springer, 2003), 1–19; quote from
p. 3.

10 So far, the sites in which "Symbiontics"
has been seeded include Olafur Eliasson,
Symbiotic Seeing, Kunsthalle Zurich (2020);
Jenna Sutela, *NO NO NSE NSE*, Kunsthall
Trondheim Norway (2020), "Virions" op. cit.
supra, Agnieszka Kurant, *Collective Intelligence*

(Sternberg Press, 2024), and various online forums. My polemic deeply respects and joins forces with Donna Haraway's "sympoiesis" and Scott F. Gilbert's "symbiopoiesis" (see below), but wants to lodge itself directly inside ontology, rather than theoretical biology. What I am after is a widespread change in cultural beliefs, not disciplinary understandings of evolution—and I take philosophy to be the driver of that change. Many thanks to my colleague Stefan Helmreich for crucial feedback on these ideas and their broader hermeneutic context.

11 Jan Sapp, "On Symbiosis, Microbes, Kingdoms, and Domains," in Bruce Clarke, ed., *Earth, Life, and System: Evolution and Ecology on a Gaian Planet* (Fordham University Press, 2015), 105–26; see also Jan Sapp, *Evolution by Association: A History of Symbiosis* (Oxford University Press, 1994). As Sapp clarifies, the term "symbiosis" was nearly simultaneously introduced by German botanist Albert Frank in 1877 (as *Symbiotismus*) and by Frenchman Anton de Bary in 1878 as *symbiosis*. Not surprisingly, both were specialists in lichens, which combine algae and fungus in a single, evolutionarily stable, mutualist entity.

12 Donna Haraway argues for "sympoiesis" not "autopoiesis" in many publications, most recently in *Staying with the Trouble: Making Kin in the Chthulucene* (Duke University Press, 2016). Her concept builds on biologist Scott Gilbert, who has made deep contributions to the scientific understanding of the evolutionary role of symbiosis, a role he and his co-authors recently name "symbiopoiesis—the codevelopment of the holobiont" over evolutionary and planetary time. See Scott F. Gilbert, Emily McDonald, Nicole Boyle, Nicholas Buttino, Lin Gyi, Mark Mai, Neelakantan Prakash, and James Robinson, "Symbiosis as a source of selectable epigenetic variation: taking the heat for the big guy," *Phil. Trans. R. Soc. B* (2010) 365, 671–78. doi:10.1098 /rstb.2009.0245.

13 Karen Barad, *Meeting the Universe Halfway: Quantum Physics and the Entanglement of Matter and Meaning* (Duke University Press, 2007).

14 I adapt this definition from the important Introduction by Bruce Clarke and Mark Hansen (2009), notably pages 9–12. They emphasize the paradox of Varela's thinking, that "the operational *closure* of autopoiesis

demands that the organism be an *open system*." The phrasing is by Evan Thompson, cited in Clarke and Hansen, 10.

15 "The interesting thing is that the magician is doing just the opposite of what most people think—hiding something. No, the magician is making things so clear that everybody can see what is going on. And that is the miracle. You must let them see the miracle, making it so convincing that absolutely nothing is hidden, nothing is under the table, everything is on the table, and that makes the whole thing very magical." Heinz von Foerster, interviewed by Bruce Clarke, in Clarke and Hansen, 32.

Earth Flag
by Aspen Mays

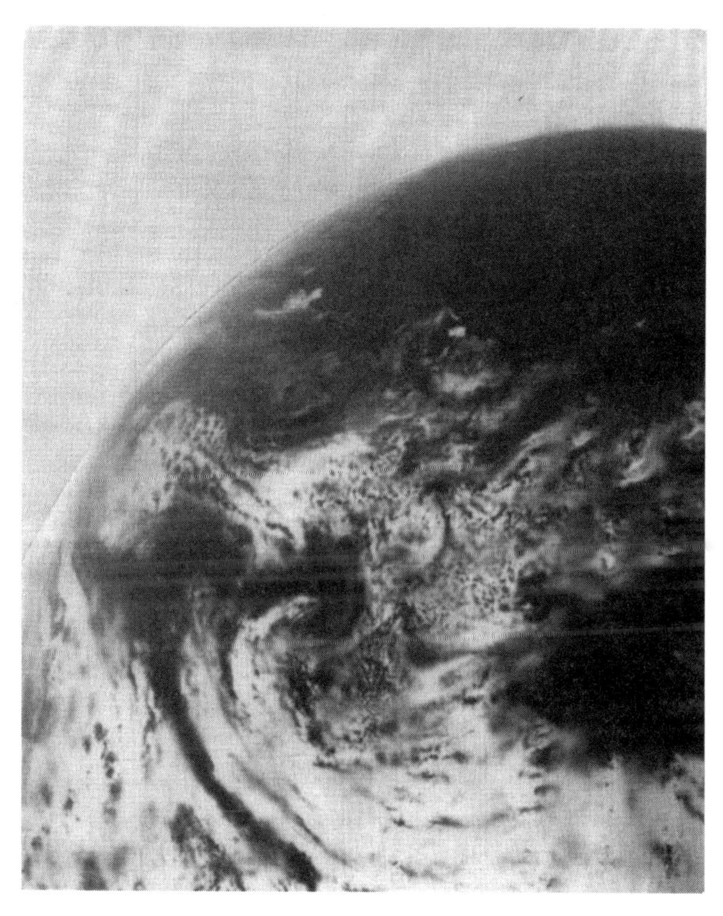

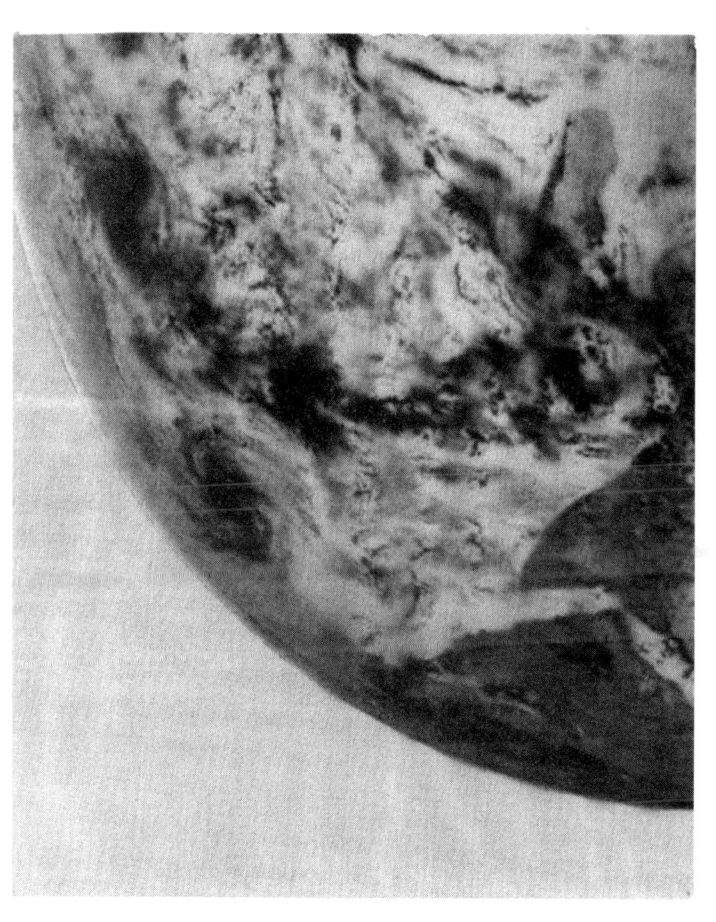

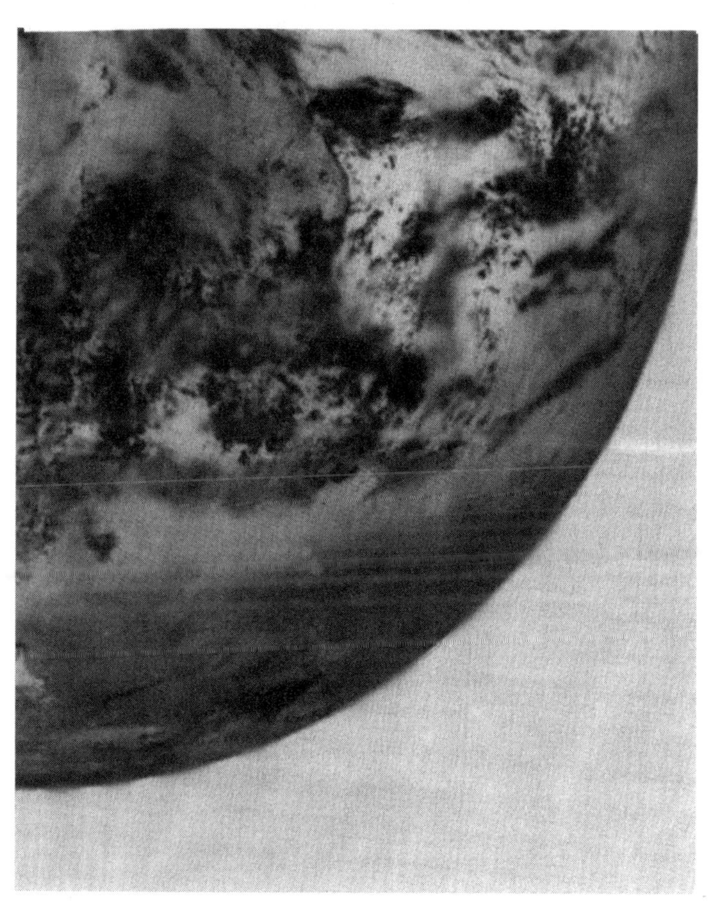

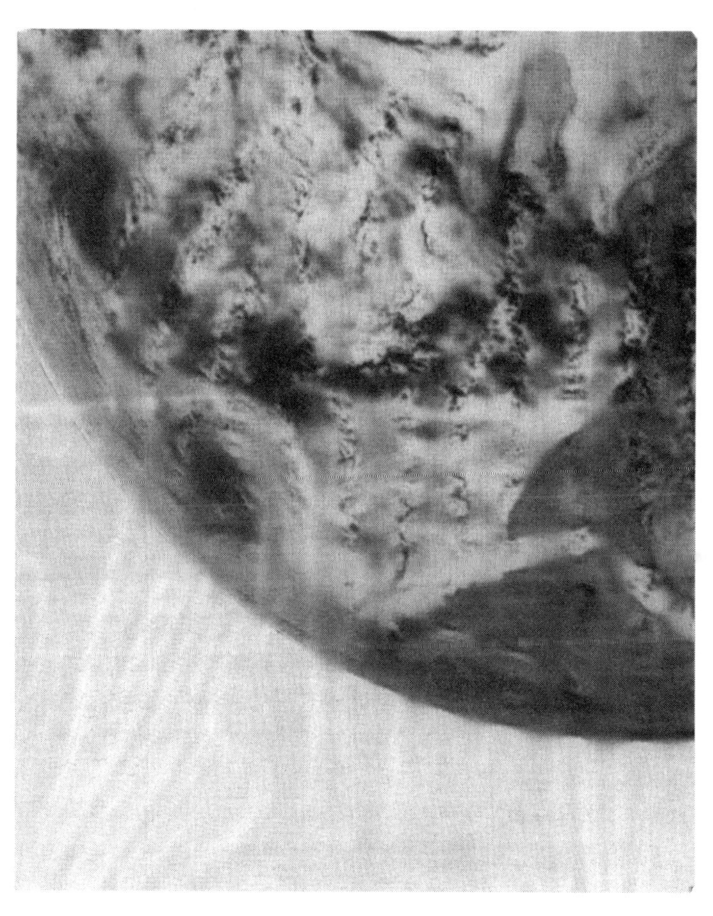

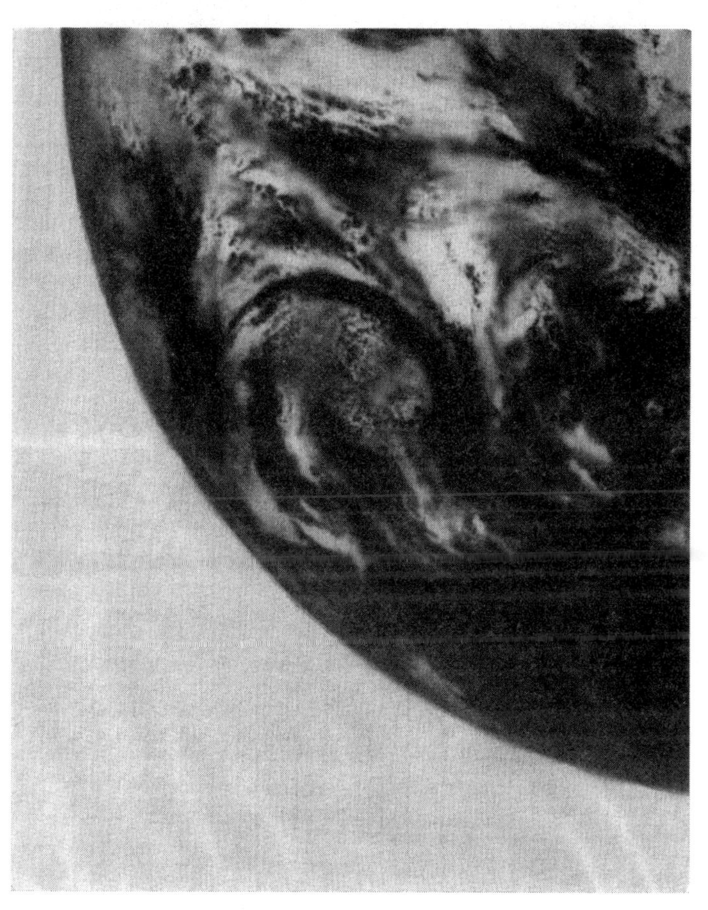

Why Look at Animals?
by John Berger

"About 1867," according to the *London Zoo Guide*, "a music hall artist called the Great Vance sang a song called *Walking in the zoo is the OK thing to do*, and the word 'zoo' came into everyday use. London Zoo also brought the word 'Jumbo' into the English language. Jumbo was an African elephant of mammoth size, who lived at the zoo between 1865 and 1882. Queen Victoria took an interest in him and eventually he ended his days as the star of the famous Barnum circus which traveled through America—his name living on to describe things of giant proportions."

Public zoos came into existence at the beginning of the period which was to see the disappearance of animals from daily life. The zoo to which people go to meet animals, to observe them, to see them, is, in fact, a monument to the impossibility of such encounters. Modern zoos are an epitaph to a relationship which was as old as man. They are not seen as such because the wrong questions have been addressed to zoos.

When they were founded—the London
Zoo in 1828, the Jardin des Plantes in 1793, the
Berlin Zoo in 1844, they brought considerable
prestige to the national capitals. The prestige
was not so different from that which had
accrued to the private royal menageries. These
menageries, along with gold plate, architecture,
orchestras, players, furnishings, dwarfs, acrobats,
uniforms, horses, art, and food, had been
demonstrations of an emperor's or king's power
and wealth. Likewise in the nineteenth century,
public zoos were an endorsement of modern
colonial power. The capturing of the animals
was a symbolic representation of the conquest of
all distant and exotic lands. "Explorers" proved
their patriotism by sending home a tiger or an
elephant. The gift of an exotic animal to the
metropolitan zoo became a token in subservient
diplomatic relations.

Yet, like every other nineteenth-century
public institution, the zoo, however supportive
of the ideology of imperialism, had to claim
an independent and civic function. The claim
was that it was another kind of museum, whose
purpose was to further knowledge and public
enlightenment. And so the first questions asked
of zoos belonged to natural history; it was then
thought possible to study the natural life of

animals even in such unnatural conditions.
A century later, more sophisticated zoologists such as Konrad Lorenz asked behavioristic and ethological questions, the claimed purpose of which was to discover more about the springs of human action through the study of animals under experimental conditions.

Meanwhile, millions visited the zoos each year out of a curiosity which was both so large, so vague, and so personal that it is hard to express in a single question. Today in France 22 million people visit the 200 zoos each year. A high proportion of the visitors were and are children.

Children in the industrialized world are surrounded by animal imagery: toys, cartoons, pictures, decorations of every sort. No other source of imagery can begin to compete with that of animals. The apparently spontaneous interest that children have in animals might lead one to suppose that this has always been the case. Certainly some of the earliest toys (when toys were unknown to the vast majority of the population) were animal. Equally, children's games, all over the world, include real or pretended animals. Yet it was not until the nineteenth century that reproductions of animals became a regular part of the decor of middle class childhoods—and then, in this century, with the advent of vast display and selling systems like Disney's—of all childhoods.

In the preceding centuries, the proportion of toys which were animal was small. And these did not pretend to realism, but were symbolic. The difference was that between a traditional hobby horse and a rocking horse: the first was merely a stick with a rudimentary head which children rode like a broom handle: the second was an elaborate "reproduction" of a horse, painted realistically, with real reins of leather, a real mane of hair, and designed movement to resemble that of a horse galloping. The rocking horse was a nineteenth-century invention.

This new demand for verisimilitude in animal toys led to different methods of manufacture. The first stuffed animals were produced, and the most expensive were covered with real animal skin—usually the skin of still-born calves. The same period saw the appearance of soft animals—bears, tigers, rabbits—such as children take to bed with them. Thus the manufacture of realistic animal toys coincides, more or less, with the establishment of public zoos.

The family visit to the zoo is often a more sentimental occasion than a visit to a fair or a football match. Adults take children to the zoo

to show them the originals of their "reproductions," and also perhaps in the hope of re-find-
ing some of the innocence of that reproduced
animal world which they remember from their
own childhood.

The animals seldom live up to the adults'
memories, whilst to the children they appear, for
the most part, unexpectedly lethargic and dull.
(As frequent as the calls of animals in a zoo, are
the cries of children demanding: Where is he?
Why doesn't he move? Is he dead?) And so one
might summarize the felt, but not necessarily
expressed question of most visitors as: Why are
these animals less than I believed?

And this unprofessional, unexpressed question is the one worth answering.

A zoo is a place where as many species and
varieties of animal as possible are collected in
order that they can be seen, observed, studied.
In principle, each cage is a frame round the
animal inside it. Visitors visit the zoo to look at
animals. They proceed from cage to cage, not
unlike visitors in an art gallery who stop in front
of one painting, and then move on to the next
or the one after next. Yet in the zoo the view is
always wrong. Like an image out of focus. One
is so accustomed to this that one scarcely notices
it any more; or, rather, the apology habitually

anticipates the disappointment, so that the latter is not felt. And the apology runs like this: What do you expect? It's not a dead object you have come to look at, it's alive. It's leading its own life. Why should this coincide with its being properly visible? Yet the reasoning of this apology is inadequate. The truth is more startling.

However you look at these animals, even if the animal is up against the bars, less than a foot from you, looking outwards in the public direction, you are looking at something that has been rendered absolutely marginal; and all the concentration you can muster will never be enough to centralize it. Why is this?

Within limits, the animals are free, but both they themselves, and their spectators, presume on their close confinement. The visibility through the glass, the spaces between the bars, or the empty air above the moat, are not what they seem—if they were, then everything would be changed. Thus visibility, space, air, have been reduced to tokens. The decor, accepting these elements as tokens, sometimes reproduces them to create pure illusion—as in the case of painted prairies or painted rock pools at the back of the boxes for small animals. Sometimes it merely adds further tokens to suggest something of the animal's original landscape—the dead branches

of a tree for monkeys, artificial rocks for bears,
pebbles and shallow water for crocodiles. These
added tokens serve two distinct purposes: for
the spectator they are like theater props: for the
animal they constitute the bare minimum of an
environment in which they can physically exist.

The animals, isolated from each other and
without interaction between species, have
become utterly dependent upon their keepers.
Consequently most of their responses have been
changed. What was central to their interest has
been replaced by a passive waiting for a series of
arbitrary outside interventions. The events they
perceive occurring around them have become as
illusory in terms of their natural responses,
as the painted prairies. At the same time this
very isolation (usually) guarantees their longevity
as specimens and facilitates their taxonomic
arrangement.

All this is what makes them marginal. The
space which they inhabit is artificial. Hence
their tendency to bundle towards the edge of it.
(Beyond its edges there may be real space.)
In some cages the light is equally artificial.
In all cases the environment is illusory. Nothing
surrounds them except their own lethargy
or hyperactivity. They have nothing to act
upon—except, briefly, supplied food and—very

occasionally—a supplied mate. (Hence their perennial actions become marginal actions without an object.) Lastly, their dependence and isolation have so conditioned their responses that they treat any event which takes place around them—usually it is in front of them, where the public is—as marginal. (Hence their assumption of an otherwise exclusively human attitude—indifference.)

Zoos, realistic animal toys, and the widespread commercial diffusion of animal imagery, all began as animals started to be withdrawn from daily life. One could suppose that such innovations were compensatory. Yet in reality the innovations themselves belonged to the same remorseless movement as was dispersing the animals. The zoos, with their theatrical decor for display, were in fact demonstrations of how animals had been rendered absolutely marginal. The realistic toys increased the demand for the new animal puppet: the urban pet. The reproduction of animals in images—as their biological reproduction in birth becomes a rarer and rarer sight—was competitively forced to make animals ever more exotic and remote.

Everywhere animals disappear. In zoos they constitute the living monument to their own disappearance. And in doing so, they provoked their last metaphor. *The Naked Ape, The Human Zoo*, are titles of world bestsellers. In these books the zoologist Desmond Morris proposes that the unnatural behavior of animals in captivity can help us to understand, accept, and overcome the stresses involved in living in consumer societies.

All sites of enforced marginalization—ghettos, shanty towns, prisons, madhouses, concentration camps—have something in common with zoos. But it is both too easy and too evasive to use the zoo as a symbol. The zoo is a demonstration of the relations between man and animals; nothing else. The marginalization of animals is today being followed by the marginalization and disposal of the only class who, throughout history, has remained familiar with animals and maintained the wisdom which accompanies that familiarity: the middle and small peasant. The basis of this wisdom is an acceptance of the dualism at the very origin of the relation between man and animal. The rejection of this dualism is probably an important factor in opening the way to modern totalitarianism. But I do not wish to go beyond the limits of that unprofessional, unexpressed but fundamental question asked of the zoo.

The zoo cannot but disappoint. The public purpose of zoos is to offer visitors the opportunity of looking at animals. Yet nowhere in a zoo can a stranger encounter the look of an animal. At the most, the animal's gaze flickers and passes on. They look sideways. They look blindly beyond. They scan mechanically. They have been immunized to encounter, because nothing can any more occupy a central place in their attention.

Therein lies the ultimate consequence of their marginalization. That look between animal and man, which may have played a crucial role in the development of human society, and with which, in any case, all men had always lived until less than a century ago, has been extinguished. Looking at each animal, the unaccompanied zoo visitor is alone. As for the crowds, they belong to a species which has at last been isolated.

This historic loss, to which zoos are a monument, is now irredeemable for the culture of capitalism.

A History of Cattle:
A Co-Species Compendium
by Brian Karl

In one of my high school biology classes held in the Southern California suburbs late in the last century, we students were told to look through a cow's eye, separated from the rest of its cow body by mortality and somebody's scalpel. The strange uncanny of the experience—grasping something out of place yet somewhat familiar, channeling vague intimations of perception—produced a sort of out-of-body experience for myself, a sense of vertigo, nausea, and borderline horror. I recall images of the world as both hazy and upside down when I put this other creature's orb as close up to my own eyeball as I dared, given the tendrils of fat and mucus-y flesh still trailing off it in tiny strands.

Growing up, I first encountered cattle at a small ranch outside of Los Angeles, a very dusty and dry place, bordered by tall eucalyptus planted as windbreaks generations earlier. My grandfather, whose main business concern was trucking alfalfa for other ranchers' animals

to fatten up on, would bring my mother and
sister and me our shares of the sides of beef he
purchased wholesale from one of his rancher
colleagues. Each animal portion was tightly
wrapped in white old-fashioned butcher
paper and stored in the small freezer atop our
refrigerator. Remembering this parceling out of
fragments of a once-whole, once-live animal into
our household brings to mind vintage "Butcher's
Guide" posters with side view images of steers
articulating different cuts of beef—a kind of
surreal dissociation of constituent body parts that
became normalized not only for me in my family
setting, but as part of a long-growing mass-scale
industry raising animals for meat for commercial
distribution.

Closer to my current Northern California
home, surrounded by fields given over to small
herds of cows allowed to roam "free" in acres
of fenced-in territory shared by humans for
hiking and by utility companies for access to
water storage and power lines, I've experienced
other uncanny episodes, near face-to-face with a
series of still living, fully embodied cows. Among
striking aspects of these encounters include the
differences between our bodies: thin-framed,
upright, two-legged primate and much larger
mammals, down on all fours. But, also different,

our circumstances: *me*, free to come and go, unlocking gates or climbing fences at will; *they*, born in the nearby landscape or delivered from outside ranches elsewhere, sometimes corralled and then picked up again by other men at various seasons for various reasons, often not exactly in accord with the cows' own motivations. You can hear this in the lowing protests they sometimes make, and the uncertain looks in their eyes.

Among striking aspects also are the challenges faced in reading the significance of various postures, movements, and expressions of cows whose paths are crossed—various combinations of curiosity, wariness, fear, and anger seem to flicker and resolve in the eyes of different animals I've met out in fields—the seasoned mothers with their large heads, massive bodies, and distended udders; the calves of different sizes who gambol and romp in play with one another and only occasionally feed at their mothers' teats while always staying nearby; and, very infrequently, full-grown bulls, since males are mostly taken away for fattening and slaughter at younger ages, save for those few kept apart for seasonal inseminations.

One rare occasion encountering an adult bull unfolded with sudden, startling awareness when one angry male emerged from among a herd of more placid females and calves to aggressively face off from thirty yards or so against a friend and me out for a walk. Pawing at the dusty ground with one determinedly forwarded hoof, the bull glared in decided rage. We humans backed away immediately, once we realized that almost cartoon-like cliché gesture signaled an imminent physical confrontation for real.

I've been charged physically two other times. Once was by another male, a half-grown adolescent seemingly friendly and curious at first, as my sister and I passed near him. His disposition shifted, though, and he began rushing at us from a couple dozen feet away, decelerating only as we hurriedly moved off in the awkwardly shared landscape. I can't blame him. Meat is murder.

It's also harsh on the environment, degrading a shared ecosystem that includes enormous amounts of methane impacting climate change, watershed runoff from chemically-loaded diets and cow poop, and carbon-intensive transport of meat to market. Cattlemen like to assert that cattle are "good" for "the environment," by which they mean the winnowing of grasses that might catch fire. Such assertions leave out how those landscapes were radically transformed in the first place by the arrival of cattle themselves, forcibly introduced by newly arriving settlers who displaced Indigenous peoples back in the mid-1800s. Formerly wild-growing or lightly cultivated areas were cleared of plant life other than what might feed cattle, and hyper-cultivated landscapes prone to erosion and humanly-induced "wild" fires became desolate and dangerous arenas serving mostly cattle and cattlemen, at the expense of other species. Not if but when humans lapse in their attempted control of the environment, what will become of hyper-bred species?

Another instance of a cow gathering momentum towards assault occurred when a mother launched herself at me from some distance—though closing the ground between us surprisingly fast—and she continued lowing angrily long after I ran off into the undergrowth of a nearby watershed ravine. Only when I emerged a quarter hour later and saw her returning from the opposite direction down a hill with a trailing juvenile did I figure out I must have come between the mother and her calf just when she'd realized her offspring was absent, wandered away out of sight.

I had witnessed several episodes of similar-aged adolescent cattle penned up in the nearby corral awaiting the arrival of a truck to cart them off for fattening and slaughter elsewhere.

These unprecedented separations affected alike mothers and children, both of whom, bewildered, bellowed impotently from different sides of the pen.

One last encounter: wandering down a ravine path, canopy overhead of high bay, buckeye, and oak trees. Talking in spurts with a companion so we don't at first register the source of a rustle in the woods nearby. A bird? A falling branch or bark? Only when we pass by, less than ten feet away, do we make out, camouflaged by leaf and branch, the surprisingly scrawny form of a lone elderly cow, staring at us in fear and apparent pain. The panic-stricken look in her eyes signals the gulf in possible understanding and aid: no matter how much compassion our meeting engenders on one side, there is a desperation that still sees antagonism from the other.

There is little we can do for her—except simply walk away and save her the extra stress of our presence. Any attempted comfort would just frighten further, adding to the pathos of her lonely immiseration. Later, a mile or so from where this sick cow has taken herself off, away from kith and kin, we reach the cow's rancher via phone, and he tells us he has already given that cow a number of medicines, hoping for, as he puts it, "one more year out of her," but now it was up to her. She was on her own.

INDEX

1
Dust jacket

The images on the dust jacket are:
*Fibre optic telecommunication cable,
(FRP-central element, plastic foil,
FRNC sheath), Ø 17mm* and *Subsea
telecommunication (coaxial twisted
screened quad, waterblock, PU sheath)
Ø 13.5mm* by Nina Canell and
Robin Watkins. Both are from the
artists' book *Mid-Sentence* (Bom Dia
Boa Tarde Boa Noite and Moderna
Museet, 2014).

2
Introduction
by Jeanne Gerrity and
Diego Villalobos

3
The Sunflower Cast a Spell to
Save Us from the Void
by Jackie Wang

This poem appears in the book
*The Sunflower Cast a Spell to Save
Us from the Void* (Nightboat Books,
2021). Copyright © 2021 by Jackie
Wang. Reprinted with permission of
Nightboat Books.

4
Umwelt & Tick
by Giorgio Agamben

This text is an excerpt from *The Open:
Man and Animal* (Stanford University
Press, 2004). *The Open* was originally
published in Italian in 2002 under
the title *L'aperto: L'uomo e l'animale*.
© 2002, Bollati Boringhieri. English
translation © 2004 by the Board of
Trustees of the Leland Stanford Junior
University.

Many thanks to Aspen Mays for
pointing us to this text.

5
A Bacterial Simulation for
Anicka Yi
by Dave Elfving

This work was commissioned for this
publication.

6
Axolotl
by Julio Cortázar

This text was first published in English
by New Directions in 1967, as part
of Cortázar's *End of the Game and
Other Short Stories*, first published in
Argentina in 1954.

7
Beetle Juice
by Pierre Huyghe

This recipe was originally published
in *Artists' Cocktails by Ryan Gander*
(Dente-De-Leon, 2013).

16
Vertical Time / Transversal Time
by Ayesha Hameed

This text is an excerpt from *Visual Cultures as Time Travel* (Sternberg Press and Goldsmiths, University of London, 2021).

17
Memoirs of a Spacewoman
by Naomi Mitchison

This text is an excerpt from *Memoirs of a Spacewoman* (Victor Gollancz Ltd., 1962).

Many thanks to Dodie Bellamy, Jackie Im, and Kyungwon Song for pointing us to this text.

18
Before It Fades
Text by Karen Cheung
Images by Heesoo Kwon

This text and accompanying images are an excerpt from *Before It Fades* (Sming Sming, 2023).

19
The Indebted
by Cathy Park Hong

This text is an excerpt from *Minor Feelings: An Asian American Reckoning* (Penguin Random House, 2020).

20
L is for Lai Teck
by Ho Tzu Nyen

This text was originally published in *HEARINGS: A READER* (Sternberg Press, 2017).

21
Sketches
by Tishan Hsu

These images are: *study – Portrait*, 1982, pencil on paper; *study – It's Not the Bullet but the Hole*, 1984, pencil and gesso on paper; *study – Vertical Ooze*, 1980, pencil on paper; *Body flow installation drawing*, 1991, pencil on paper; *Rippling tile surface sketch*, 1980, pencil on paper. Copyright © Tishan Hsu Artists Rights Society / New York. All Rights Reserved.

Please note that the original drawings are in color.

22
Toxic Worlding
by Mel Y. Chen

This text is an excerpt from *Animacies: Biopolitics, Racial Mattering, and Queer Affect*, 189–221. Copyright ©2012, Duke University Press. All rights reserved. Republished by permission of the copyright holder, and the Publisher. www.dukeupress.edu.

23
INITIAL PUBLIC OFFERING
OOOO (IPOOOOO)
by Jen Liu

These images are: *Us vs. Them*, 2012, ink on paper, 53 × 53 inches; *Orestes and Elektra*, 2012, ink on paper, 92 × 55 inches; *One With You*, 2012, ink on paper, 30 × 22 inches; *Together We're Stronger*, 2012, ink on paper, 30 × 22 inches; *Hello Future*, 2012, ink on paper, 30 × 22 inches; *Master O-Note*, 2012, ink on paper, 92 × 55 inches. Courtesy of the artist, Upstream Gallery, Amsterdam, and Blindspot Gallery, Hong Kong.

24
Symbiontics: a view of present
conditions from a place of
entanglement
by Caroline A. Jones

This essay was originally published in *The Brooklyn Rail* (Jul–Aug 2020).

25
Earth Flag
by Aspen Mays

These gelatin silver photograms were commissioned for this publication.

26
Why Look at Animals?
by John Berger

This text is an excerpt from *About Looking* (Pantheon Books, 1980).

Many thanks to Brian Karl for pointing us to this text.

27
A History of Cattle:
A Co-Species Compendium
by Brian Karl

This work was commissioned for this publication.

28
Tulip and Aphids
Jochen Lempert

The image is: *Tulip and Aphids*, 2013, silver gelatin print, 24 × 18 cm. Courtesy of the artist, ProjecteSD, Barcelona and BQ, Berlin.

—

Every effort has been made to trace copyright holders and to ensure that all the information present is correct. If proper copyright acknowledgment has not been made, or for clarifications and corrections, please contact the publishers, and we will correct the information in future reprintings.

Most texts retain the spelling and capitalization of the original publications.

Does the sun have a translucent shell?
(A Series of Open Questions, vol. 5)

Published by CCA Wattis Institute for Contemporary Arts
and Sternberg Press

Editors: Jeanne Gerrity & Diego Villalobos
Design: Scott Ponik*
Editorial Assistant: Addy Rabinovitch
Proofreader: Vanessa Kauffman Zimmerly

Printed and bound by Friesens (Manitoba), in an edition of 1500
Printed on Glatfelter Exbulk 50 lb.
Set in Janson Text

ISBN 978-1-915609-73-1

Distributed by The MIT Press, Art Data, and Les presses du réel

This book, the fifth volume of the Wattis Institute's annual A Series of Open
Questions readers, is a result of a year of learning from the work of Anicka Yi
in the company of research group members Nilgun Bayraktar, Dave Elfving,
Susie Fu, Taro Hattori, Jackie Im, Brian Karl, Aspen Mays, and Kyungwon Song,
with assistance by Paulina Félix Cunillé. Special thanks to Anicka Yi
and Remina Greenfield.

CCA Wattis Institute for Contemporary Arts
145 Hooper Street
San Francisco, CA 94107
www.wattis.org

Sternberg Press
71–75 Shelton Street
UK–London WC2H 9JQ
www.sternberg-press.com

Robin Beard, Head of Installation & Exhibition Design; Paulina Félix Cunillé, Curatorial Research Assistant; Jeanne Gerrity, Deputy Director & Director of Programs; Armaan Mumtaz, Gallery Associate; Daisy Nam, Zlot Family Director & Chief Curator; Addy Rabinovitch, Operations Coordinator; Carolyn Salcido, Head of Membership & Senior Director, CCA Advancement; Diego Villalobos, Associate Curator

Wattis Assistants: Samantha Hiura, Heather Leighton, Akhil Nalluri, Majdah Omer

The CCA Wattis Institute program is generously supported by Mary and Harold Zlot, the Grants for the Arts / San Francisco Hotel Tax Fund, and The Horace W. Goldsmith Foundation; by Leadership contributors Jonathan Gans and Abigail Turin, and Katie and Matt Paige; by Carlie Wilmans; and by CCA Wattis Institute's Curator's Forum members. Phyllis C. Wattis was the generous founding patron.

This reader is the fifth volume of an annual publication series, A Series of Open Questions.

*Following *Walking on Splinters*; published by Werkplaats Typografie, Arnhem, the Netherlands, 2004; edited and designed by Marijke Cobbenhagen, Joana Katte, Louis Lüthi, Janna Meeus, Radim Peško, Willi Schmid, and Maxine Kopsa. Thanks to Anniek Brattinga, Armand Mevis, and Maxine Kopsa.

Printed in Canada

Tulip and Aphids
by Jochen Lempert

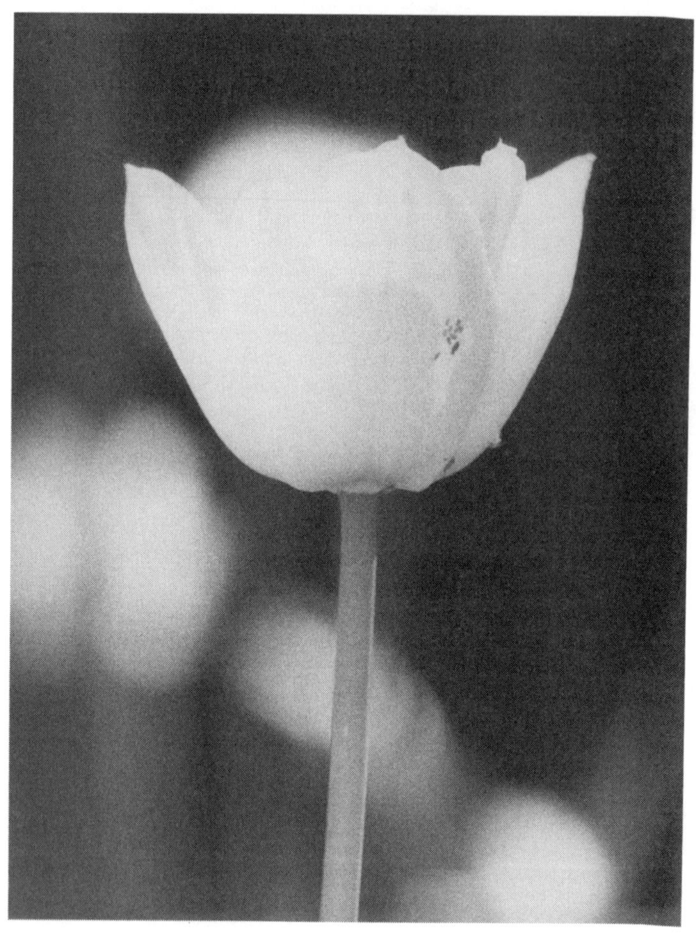